5|03

The Catcher in the Rye

PETER LANG
New York • Washington, D.C./Baltimore • Bern
Frankfurt am Main • Berlin • Brussels • Vienna • Oxford

The Catcher in the Rye

New Essays

EDITED BY
J. P. Steed

PETER LANG
New York • Washington, D.C./Baltimore • Bern
Frankfurt am Main • Berlin • Brussels • Vienna • Oxford

Library of Congress Cataloging-in-Publication Data

The catcher in the Rye: new essays / edited by J. P. Steed.
p. cm.
Includes bibliographical references and index.
1. Salinger, J. D. (Jerome David), 1919— Catcher in the rye.
2. Caulfield, Holden (Fictitious character) 3. Runaway teenagers in literature.
4. Teenage boys in literature. I. Steed, J. P.
PS3537.A426 C3226   813'.54—dc21   2001038487
ISBN 0-8204-5729-9

Die Deutsche Bibliothek-CIP-Einheitsaufnahme

The catcher in the rye: new essays / ed. by: J. P. Steed.
−New York; Washington, D.C./Baltimore; Bern;
Frankfurt am Main; Berlin; Brussels; Vienna; Oxford: Lang.
ISBN 0-8204-5729-9

Cover design by Lisa Dillon

The paper in this book meets the guidelines for permanence and durability
of the Committee on Production Guidelines for Book Longevity
of the Council of Library Resources.

Printed in the United States of America

Contents

Introduction:
The Catcher in the Rye at Fifty, 1951–2001

J. P. STEED

One can only presume that it is the fiftieth anniversary of *The Catcher in the Rye* that has occasioned a resurgence in the attention being given to Salinger's novel among readers, teachers, scholars, critics, and publishers. Recent customers at the local bookstore superchain have found copies of Salinger's books prominently displayed on the end of an aisle; a book on Salinger's fiction by John Unrue and a collection of "Letters to Salinger" are both forthcoming; Sanford Pinsker recently wrote a short piece entitled "Holden on Social Security" for the *Washington Times*; and David Rachels, in the *Chronicle of Higher Education*, has admonished academia to promote *Catcher* from the ranks of "high-school book" to that held by *Huckleberry Finn*, as "college book (that is sometimes taught in high school)." All in all, the Salinger industry—as it has been called—seems to have received an injection of new life in its golden age. The present volume seeks to be both a component and a beneficiary of this injection and hopes to become a substantial part of the critical discourses of J. D. Salinger, American literary studies, and American cultural studies. And its primary intent is to demonstrate and to interrogate *Catcher*'s relevance to American literature and culture, regardless of any sense of its hierarchical status—which is to say that we are concerned with *The Catcher in the Rye* itself, and its relevance to American literature and culture, and we are *not* concerned with this relevance as it is compared to the relevance of some other work. Despite George Steiner's early relegation of Salinger to the status of "good minor writer" and despite the attempts by some Salinger scholars to throw off that label, we are not concerned with how "major" or "minor" Salinger is. If there is one thing the past fifty years of literary theory and criticism have taught us, it is that such questions are utterly subjective and eventually meaningless.

However, thanks primarily to Steiner's premature proclamation and to a certain anxiety extant among those who choose to write about Salinger (while sitting in an office on the same floor as those who write about Twain, Shakespeare, Hardy, and Chaucer), it is apparently impossible to acknowledge the passing of *Catcher*'s first fifty years without saying something about its status among American novels. Pinsker, in his *Washington Times* article, claimed Holden "continues to be the (anti-)hero of choice for one generation of adolescents after another" and pointed to book sales, asserting that *Catcher* "has probably posted higher sales figures than any other serious American novel." And Rachels's article in the *Chronicle* concerns itself entirely with the endeavor to elevate *Catcher* to a more "major" rung on the literary ladder—represented, for Rachels, by a more widespread use of the novel in university classrooms. Steiner made his assessment of Salinger when *Catcher* was maybe half as old as its own protagonist. It appears that, with the novel being now a half a century old, a reassessment is in order.

Allowing for the relatively small quantity of his work, then, and thus accepting Steiner's ranking as quantitatively true, it nevertheless seems qualitatively true that in American literature there is no more major minor writer than J. D. Salinger. Salinger's creations—the Glass family, little Esmé, Teddy McArdle, Mary Jane and Eloise, Chief John Gedsudski—have continued to enthrall readers for decades now, and amazingly they have managed to do so despite their conspicuous absence from the myriad anthologies of literature that play so dominant a role in shaping our canons and curriculums and in manipulating our readerly appetites. Indeed, Salinger's attempts to withhold his creations from us seem only to titillate our interest in them, to arouse our attraction to them—as though Salinger has pulled off a calculated literary striptease. And, of course, here I am referring only to the "minor" creations of this "minor" writer. Clearly, with none of Salinger's creations have we felt a stronger affinity than Holden Caulfield, that precocious, romantically cynical, cynically romantic teenager who—in all his Americanness—often embodies that which he criticizes, while nobly grasping (and perpetually failing) to protect that which he idealizes. In 1951's post-World War II, pre-Civil Rights Movement America, Holden Caulfield—do we dare say single-handedly?—(re)defined the identity of the American teenager and subsequently reconstructed the identity of Americans.

That's a fairly major contribution coming from someone pegged as merely a "good minor writer."

Despite this contribution, though, and perhaps because of Salinger's unfading popularity, especially among younger readers, Salinger's novel has continued to live under the shadow of Steiner's indictment. But the fact is, when compared to Salinger, no other one-novel writer can lay claim to a creation that has so thoroughly permeated American popular culture as has Salinger's Holden Caulfield. One must look to the bona fide "major" writers such as Mark Twain to find a figure (in Huck Finn) who can even come close to competing with Holden for the prize of Fictional Character Most Inculcated into American Social Consciousness. Why, even from among these so-called "major" writers, Twain may be the only legitimate competitor. None of Hemingway's or Faulkner's characters come close, and Melville, Poe and Hawthorne can offer perhaps only a whale, a beating heart, and a letter of the alphabet, respectively.

But rather than continue down this pathway of controversial and essentially meaningless competitions and comparisons—a path I have already traversed longer than I had intended—I will desist. (And I will note that it is an unfortunate consequence that in the attention to or elevation of the one there must always be the implicit or explicit diminishment or marginalization of the other.) Despite the hyperbolic and albeit only somewhat facetious assertions made above, the ultimate intent here is not to diminish the contributions of other writers in comparing them to Salinger or to set Salinger above them in some reorganized literary hierarchy. Perhaps this momentary lapse can be chalked up to that certain anxiety I mentioned; entire semester-long courses are being devoted to Hemingway and Faulkner, down the hall from here, while I rely on Rachels's *Chronicle* article as justification for the inclusion of *Catcher* in a general course on fiction.

All anxieties and facetiousness aside, however, and as it has been previously stated, we are not concerned with how "major" or "minor" Salinger is. In all seriousness, if there is one thing the past fifty years of literary theory and criticism have taught us, it is that such questions are utterly subjective and eventually meaningless.

And you will see that in the essays that follow, this question is ignored, abandoned. Mark Silverberg's essay, "'You Must Change Your Life': Formative Responses to *The Catcher in the Rye*," supplies a brief history of the Salinger industry and of the various reactions to *Catcher* and its impact on the literary scene; but aside from this account, which does touch on Salinger's comparative popularity and so forth, nowhere outside this introduction does the question of comparative status preoccupy the author. Silverberg's essay is concerned instead with the "complicated, messy, and sometimes volatile interaction that occurs between text and reader" and takes *Catcher*—a novel which has been known to elicit what Silverberg calls the "formative response"—as its principal specimen for examination.

In "Mentor Mori; or, Sibling Society and the *Catcher* in the Bly," Robert Miltner also ignores *Catcher* as "major" or "minor" novel and instead focuses on *Catcher* as sociological artifact. Using Robert Bly's *Sibling Society* and *Iron John* as lenses, Miltner examines Holden's familial relationships and, in turn, the adolescent experience in 1950s America.

Intertextual studies then take center stage, as Dennis Cutchins and Joseph S. Walker both examine the relationship(s) between and the confluence of a variety of texts: namely, the written texts of *Catcher* and W. P. Kinsella's *Shoeless Joe*; the film- or image-text of *Field of Dreams* (the movie version of Kinsella's novel); and the cultural-text of J. D. Salinger-as-myth or as cultural commodity.

Finally, Matt Evertson's "Love, Loss and Growing up in J. D. Salinger and Cormac McCarthy" is a comparative, intertextual study of two American novels addressing similar themes. Evertson cites the frequent comparison of Holden Caulfield to Huckleberry Finn and then extends this literary genealogy to John Grady, the protagonist of McCarthy's *All the*

Pretty Horses, claiming a similar kinship between *Catcher* and *Horses* and noting that

> while the telling of these stories has changed…the importance of the storytelling itself has not. Both books burst with the sense of the need to explain, to share the loss, disillusion and disappointments…that comprise the universal experience of growing up.

And so it is that with these five essays this volume demonstrates that—while arguments over Salinger's relative status among American authors and the status of *The Catcher in the Rye* among American novels might continue unresolved and unabated for another fifty years, regardless of however subjective and meaningless those arguments might be—there is no arguing the continuing relevance of Salinger and his novel to American literature and culture. In closing, and as further evidence, we might note that, had this volume been compiled six months later than it was, we surely would have found references to the recent movie *Finding Forrester* (2000)—a film about a reclusive one-hit-novel author who is coaxed out of reclusion by a troubled teenager who wishes to preserve or to assert some integrity in a corrupted world. As such, the film clearly becomes yet another example of the pervasiveness of the (here) conflated myths of Salinger and Holden Caulfield and illustrates again the prominence of the two within American culture. Despite the cries of "major" versus "minor" that permeate all aspects of Salinger discourse, it would appear that—just as one cannot wholly resist or refute that controversy—one likewise cannot resist or refute the argument that, after fifty years, our interest in and attraction to the Salinger industry has not waned. Or, as Sanford Pinsker puts it, though Holden is now old enough to qualify for Social Security, undeniably, irresistibly, "the novel's power still lives on."

October 22, 2001

1.

"You Must Change Your Life": Formative Responses to *The Catcher in the Rye*

MARK SILVERBERG

The Formative Summons

What exactly do readers mean when they say "I fell in love with that book" or "It changed my life"? This essay is concerned with what I will call the formative summons of a work of art, the voice which seems to compel readers to "change their lives" as in the final line of Rilke's famous poem on the "Archaic Torso of Apollo." Such a command is one which many readers have heard but which critical discourse has rarely discussed. A perfect example of such a summons occurs in one of the most poignant moments of the John Lennon documentary, *Imagine*. In this scene, one of Lennon's assistants brings an uninvited guest to meet the rock star outside his estate in Ascot, England. The soiled and somewhat deranged-looking visitor, who apparently has been sleeping in the garden of Lennon's large property for days, stares at his idol in a combination of awe and utter confusion. In half-coherent sentences, the man explains that he needed to find the singer because Lennon's songs were written for him. "I figured if we met, I'd *know* just by meeting you," he says. He tries to explain how the songs are about him, about his life, how they say the things he feels but is unable to articulate. What the visitor implies is that the songs have given him a life—that they speak not only to him but *for* him.

Lennon spends some time trying to explain that in fact the songs are about *his* life, about his and Yoko's relationship, and sometimes, Lennon continues, the songs are only word games:

...literally nonsense. ...You just take words and stick them together and see if
they have any meaning. Some of them do, some of them don't. ...Don't confuse
the songs with your own life. They may have relevance to your own life, but a lot
of things do.

This reasoning makes little sense to the visitor, who stares in blank
confusion, occasionally interjecting a line—"you weren't thinking of anyone
in particular when you wrote those songs?" The scene ends, fittingly, not
with any realization on the visitor's part but with Lennon inviting him into
the house for something to eat.

The power of this scene derives in part from the unmistakable *cinéma
vérité* quality of the moment—the unstaged confusion and pain of the visitor
and Lennon's hopeless, though well-intentioned, attempts to explain his
music. As well, the real poignancy of this moment, I think, derives from the
fact that many people, with some slight stretch of the imagination, can put
themselves in the visitor's place. On some basic level it is not hard to
identify with the visitor and with the feeling of being summoned by a text.
How many of us cannot recall feeling, particularly during adolescence, that
a text—whether a song, a novel, or a poem—was speaking directly,
privately, and intimately to us? This is the familiar, though untheorized,
response of those who make comments such as "I fell in love with that
book"; "it became a part of me"; or "it changed my life." Such a response
probably remains untheorized because it seems the epitome of critical
naiveté—it confuses literature with life in the most flagrant ways. Is it not,
after all, the response of the vagrant who believes John Lennon is writing
songs about him or of the impressionable adolescent who believes he must
change his life based on the commands of Ayn Rand? The business of
literary criticism has given little place to this kind of emotional response,
and yet I believe that it is primary—both in the sense of being an initial
untutored reaction, and in the sense of being an essential, powerful
response from which later "sophisticated" responses develop. The purpose
of this essay is to examine the nature of this formative encounter by
focusing on an author and a novel which have arguably elicited a formative

response more often, and more forcefully, than any other work of literature of the twentieth century: J. D. Salinger's *The Catcher in the Rye*.

Mapping the Salinger Industry

It seems to be a ritual of the large body of Salinger criticism to begin with a numerical or descriptive account of Salinger's continued, and admittedly remarkable, popularity. Since *The Catcher in the Rye*'s publication in 1951, five generations of critics have been amazed, repulsed, and fascinated by Salinger's extraordinary popularity. The initial reviews of *Catcher* established the partisan lines along which the novel would be discussed for several decades. On the positive side, the *New York Times* reviewer, Nash Burger, proclaimed the book "strange and wonderful...an unusually brilliant first novel" (19), while the *Chicago Sunday Tribune* called it "engaging and believable...full of right observation and sharp insight" (Engle 3). On the negative side, some critics disparaged Salinger, but more often they condemned his young narrator. The *Christian Science Monitor* found the novel "a nightmarish medley of loneliness, bravado, and supineness...wholly repellent in its mingled vulgarity, naivete, and sly perversion" (Longstreth 30), while the Montreal *Gazette* condemned Holden as an "unappealing young neurotic" (Rodriquez 25). Finally, Anne Goodman in the *New Republic* ends what appears to be a lukewarm review, wherein she chastises Salinger and his creation for precocious cleverness, with a surprisingly conciliatory conclusion. "*The Catcher in the Rye* is a brilliant tour-de-force," she writes, "but in a writer of Salinger's undeniable talent one expects something more" (Salzberg 24). The strong reactions of these early reviews set a reading climate and also foreshadowed the extreme attraction and repulsion the novel would engender.

Whether for good or ill, Salinger was a hot item. By 1959 Arthur Mizener noted in *Harper's* that Salinger was "probably the most avidly read author of any serious pretensions of his generation" (Salzman 1). George Steiner took a slightly different tack in the same year when he complained

bitterly of the "pomposities and exaggerations" of "The Salinger Industry."
In an article in *The Nation*, Steiner coined the much-reused term "The
Salinger Industry" to describe the plethora of essays turned out on this, in
the critic's estimation, minor writer. To Steiner, Salinger is an "entertaining
writer…[with] a marvelous ear for the semi-literate meanderings of the
adolescent mind…" whose great success comes from his ability to "flatter
the very ignorance and moral shallowness of his young readers" (115–16).
Steiner concludes that the mass of Salinger articles are produced simply for
self-promotion rather than to fulfill the responsibilities of serious criticism
and that this has led to "a gross devaluation of standards" (118). Whether
we find Steiner's complaints justified or not is of no great concern here;
what is more important is that Steiner felt these complaints were necessary
as an antidote to Salinger's burgeoning popularity—not only among "semi-
literate" adolescents but also in the critical establishment.

Steiner's reservations aside, Salinger's popularity grew to its height in
the sixties when *Catcher* became an established part of high school and
university curricula. For a growing faction of adolescents, the novel had
become, in Ian Hamilton's phrase, "the indispensable manual from which
cool styles of disaffection could be borrowed" (155). Robert Gutwillig's
1961 article, "Everybody's Caught *The Catcher in the Rye*," in the *New York
Times Book Review* began by noting both *Catcher*'s astounding sales figures
(1.5 million copies in the United States alone), and its adoption by "Yale,
Northern Baptist Theological Seminary and 275 other colleges and
universities across the country…as required or supplementary reading" (1).
By the end of the 60s, *Facts on File* (1968) proclaimed *Catcher* "one of the
leading 25 bestsellers since 1895" (Sublette 132).

Though the seventies may have seen some slackening in the Salinger
Industry, the novel continued to sell remarkably and to interest a core of
critic-fans. In another form of the Industry, Richard Davidson happily
noted the continued enthusiasm at a special Salinger session of the 1977
MLA convention in Chicago, where three of the panelists were working on
book-length studies of Salinger (1).[1] The 1970s also saw John Romano's
suspiciously dubbed "reappraisal" of Salinger in the *New York Times Review*

of Books. Romano hoped to resuscitate a reputation that he believed was in peril, arguing that

> It's nostalgia, as a matter of fact, that can keep us from seeing and saying that Salinger is one of the very best living writers; because to say so convincingly, we must free ourselves from the benign, patronizing formulas by which we usually count him merely a good one. Salinger is a victim not of neglect but of our careless, unrecast affection. (10)

Romano makes essentially the same argument as Steiner—pitting popularity against value—though in an inverse way. Where Steiner maintains critics have inflated Salinger's import, confusing popularity with value, Romano argues that critics and other readers have devalued Salinger because of his popularity. What emerges from these discussions finally is not a measure of Salinger's "objective" value but the indication that a great part of his abiding importance is inextricably tied to his continuing popularity.

In the eighties, Mary Suzanne Schriber began her astute feminist reading of the Salinger phenomenon by noting: "If Holden Caulfield set out to study the criticism of *The Catcher in the Rye*, he would find himself...the subject, by 1981, of 344 essays and reviews, 21 books, 142 references and articles and chapters, and 14 dissertations and theses in the United States alone" (226). Though the Salinger boom may have died down, critics in the 70s and 80s were at no loss to find new perspectives from which to read Salinger. Freudian, Marxist, Buddhist, Lacanian, Alderian, intertextual, structuralist, feminist, and deconstructive readings (to name a few) have all been produced. Likewise in the 90s, over twenty-five years after Salinger published his last story, interest in Salinger continued unabated. Two new collections of essays on *Catcher* were published by G. K. Hall and Cambridge in 1990 and '91, and in 1999 Sanford and Ann Pinsker produced the "Student Casebook," *Understanding The Catcher in the Rye*. Far from being extinct, the Salinger Industry seems to have set up a branch plant in Japan where numerous articles, reviews, books, and theses have been produced in the last decade.[2] By 1981, both Japan and Russia had no less than half a dozen translated versions of *Catcher* (Sublette 216, 222).

Holden and Salinger have long ago moved beyond the boundaries of formal literary discourse, where New Critical approaches sometimes sought to contain them. Although rarely seen on university curricula, the novel remains a fixture in high school English classrooms in North America and abroad. As well, Holden has been enshrined in history textbooks, such as *A History of the United States Since 1945*, where he is seen as much as a sociological and historical entity as a literary character. As if in direct opposition to Salinger's intentional disappearing act, the author's name has become a permanent component of American culture. The eighties and nineties have seen Salinger revived and re-imagined in a host of fictional and semi-fictional discourses. For example, Salinger's self-imposed exile might be read under the disguise of Don DeLillo's reclusive writer in *Mao II*. Or, at the opposite extreme, readers have seen Salinger returned to the world from his mythical displacement in W. P. Kinsella's bestseller *Shoeless Joe*. Ian Hamilton's unauthorized and appropriately titled biography, *In Search of J. D. Salinger*, brings readers little new information about Salinger-the-man but does much to extend the range of Salinger-the-myth. Throughout the 1990s, Salinger's name and presence reappeared in television sitcoms such as *Mad About You* and *The Single Guy*. The darker side of the Salinger phenomenon is re-conceptualized in John Guare's 1990 drama *Six Degrees of Separation*, where Paul's fascination with Holden and *Catcher* (on which the character claims to be writing his Harvard thesis) leads him to create a Salinger-like text of his imaginary life which eventuates in catastrophe. One of the "texts" which informs Guare's work, and in fact might be deemed a primary cultural text of the eighties, is the shocking real-life document created in 1980 when Mark Chapman, carrying a copy of *Catcher* inscribed "*This* is my statement," shot and killed John Lennon. All of these texts, as well as the more recent highly sensational autobiographies by Joyce Maynard and Margaret Salinger, indicate the remarkably abiding popularity and influence of Salinger and his most famous novel.

A Case History of Us All?

All of these numeric and descriptive accounts of Salinger's popularity lead to one simple question: Why? Why have so many people been compelled to contemplate, imitate, analyze, and reconstruct this novel over so many years? The answer to this question takes us back to John Lennon's uninvited visitor. I believe that like Lennon's caller, a large number of people have felt themselves summoned by and to *The Catcher in the Rye*. Lennon's visitor believed that the songs were about him. In other words, he *identified* with the songs. This seems plain enough and also seems crucially related to the *Catcher* phenomenon, for from the very beginning of its reception reviewers talked about how they, and countless young readers, identified with Holden. Ernest Jones, Freud's pupil and biographer, set the tone for these identification comments by entitling his 1951 review of *Catcher* in *The Nation* "Case History of All of Us." Jones found Salinger's novel "predictable and boring" because it simply recorded "something not at all rich and strange but what every sixteen-year-old since Rousseau has felt, and of course what each of us is certain he has felt" (24).

Based on the experience of their own students, numerous teachers have agreed that the novel encapsulates what "every" young person has felt. High school teacher Alvin Alley writes: "Every student of mine who has read *Catcher in the Rye*...has readily identified himself with its hero, Holden Caulfield. They see in him, not the ideal young man, but a young man in search of himself, in search of his place in the human scheme of things..." (16–17). Similar articles by teachers, both male and female, such as Bernard Kinnick's "Holden Caulfield: Adolescents' Enduring Model," and Nancy Ralston's "Holden Caulfield: Super-Adolescent," have reinforced Alley's point. The frequency with which this universalizing gesture is made (equating Holden's experience with "everybody's" experience) suggests several facts. The first is that clearly a lot of people *have* identified with the novel, and with Holden's experience in particular. As we will see, many of Holden's feelings—in particular, his pervasive anxiety and uncertainty—are prototypical of adolescent experience as described by such leading experts as Erik Erikson and Anna Freud. As well, perhaps because of the (sometimes extreme) anxiety of youth, some readers no doubt find comfort in the belief that their own experience is shared by a community of respondents. This community is sometimes exaggerated into "everyone" as a way of validating the young reader's own feelings: "What I feel may seem troubled and strange," the reader tacitly implies, "but in fact it's perfectly normal; it's what *everyone* feels."

It is worth noting that another group of readers validate their identification with Holden in exactly the *opposite* way. These readers feel that their experience and Holden's experience are special because they are *unique*. In this case, the anxiety and disaffection of youth is a rare understanding shared between Holden and the reader. Holden's testament or story thus forms a special pact or bond between character and reader—only he and I understand it—while the rest of the phony slobs out there would never "get" it. Readers who identify in this way would never suggest that Holden's experience is shared by "everyone"—rather, it must be unique to "Holden and me." I suspect that this kind of identification is most typical of adolescent readers, whereas the suggestion that Holden's experience belongs to "everyone" is a typical adult strategy for rationalizing or explaining the feelings of their youth. Significantly, this universalizing gesture is often made by high school teachers, whose job it is to work in close contact with adolescents but who also must maintain a professional distance from adolescence. This distance might be maintained by universalizing, and hence standardizing, adolescent experience. Such a gesture makes Holden's experience, and adolescent experience in general, safe to work with and to teach. One can make teachable generalizations about abstracted and generalized experience, whereas individual, intensely felt emotion has a messy, unteachable quality about it.

In the field of *Catcher* criticism, a remarkably diverse group of voices have commented on the issue of identification. Many pronouncements have been made in a formal, supposedly objective discourse typified by James E. Miller's highly regarded study, *J. D. Salinger*.

> Holden Caulfield, the fumbling adolescent nauseated by the grossness of the world's body, may be the characteristic hero of contemporary fiction and the modern world. There can be no doubt that for today's American youth, Holden is an embodiment of their secret terrors and their accumulated hostilities, their slender joys and their magnified agonies. (20)

A less formal discourse, though one with no less pretension to objectivity, is heard among reviewers for journals such as *New York Times Review of Books*:

> What was it about the novel that struck Americans so squarely ten years ago and continues to hit the mark still? Primarily it was, I think, the shock of recognition. Many of my friends and this writer himself identified completely with Holden.... After reading the novel several of us went out and bought ourselves red caps with earflaps, and we all took to calling each other "Ace" and "Prince." (Gutwillig 5)

Finally, the least formal, often unashamedly subjective accounts of identification come from perhaps the most interesting source: adolescents themselves. Christopher Parker's appropriately titled "Why the Hell *Not* Smash All the Windows?," presents "a crazy kid's view of a crazy kid":

> I knew at least ten Holden Caulfields at ITT.... I think Caulfield's issue is a very real one—strong—and lets every boy who reads *The Catcher* think he's just like Holden and I think that's one of the reasons for its great success; we can all identify ourselves with his plight.... It's also sort of a fad among us to be very critical of everything and everyone, and those who are most critical are the strongest and most independent. (280–1)

All of these comments seems straightforward enough, but what they hide, behind the easy shorthand afforded by the word "identification," is an extremely troublesome critical problem. While "identification" may be a useful catchword for reviews, personal anecdotes, and generalizations about *Catcher*, it remains an entirely problematic term for critical inquiry. In *Identity: Youth and Crisis*, Erik Erikson provides an argument for why this may be so:

> The fact is that identification as a mechanism is of limited usefulness. Children at different stages of their development identify with those part aspects of people by which they themselves are most immediately affected, whether in reality or fantasy. Their identifications with parents, for example, center in certain overvalued and ill-understood body parts, capacities, and role appearances. (158)

The term "identification" is misleading because it often leads to too great a preoccupation with the other at the expense of the self. Following Erikson's logic (which follows Freud's), we "identify" with those things which most immediately and intimately cause internal effects (usually positive feelings). Then, in a process which we call "identification," we project those effects (our own feelings) onto the other which we believe to be their source. Hence, in the case of the child, there is identification with the mother or father, because the parent provides gratification of essential needs. In the case of the reader, he or she identifies with "Holden" (or any other character) because in reading Holden's story certain positive internal feelings are produced. Hence the reader says "I identify with Holden because he is sensitive and intelligent," rather than the more accurate statement: "I identify with Holden because *he makes me feel* sensitive and intelligent." Identification, then, is finally and foremost about the self (for our purposes, the reader). Reviewers and respondents, however, as we shall see, have traditionally sought the meaning of their identifications in the text rather than in themselves. In what follows I want to look at the way certain readers' putative analyses of the text turn out to be, simultaneously, analyses of themselves.

Formative Books or Formative Responses?

We turn now to the one critic who has made some attempt to theorize the process of identification with, and the "formativity" of, *The Catcher in the Rye*. Sanford Pinsker's 1986 article *"The Catcher in the Rye and All: Is the Age of Formative Books Over?"* is presented as "an attempt, admittedly autobiographical, to talk about certain connections between reading and culture—not as a 'reader-response' theorist, not as a statistics-and-graph sociologist, but rather as one who fell in love with *The Catcher in the Rye* early, and who has been trying to figure out what that has meant ever since" (953). Although Pinsker begins by foregrounding his own subjectivity, his argument quickly turns to statements of objectivity. Rather than seeking the meaning of his "falling in love" within himself, Pinsker posits its meaning within the text. Hence, as the critic's title suggests, *Catcher* is viewed as a "formative book"—a book which in its greatness (or formativity, to coin a new word) *causes* the reader to fall in love with it. Pinsker suggests that the text spoke for him, that it knew him better than he knew himself: "Holden …gives eloquent expression to what I could not have articulated myself" (954).

Pinsker goes on to elucidate some of the qualities of "formative" books. Such novels are able to capture universal truths but also to clothe them in culturally and historically specific costumes (954). Furthermore, formative books seize the imagination at exactly that moment when it is most vulnerable and voracious (955). Finally, formative books—like trees falling with a thundering crash in an unpopulated forest—seem capable of existing without readers. "The truth is," Pinsker writes, "that our formative books survive not only subsequent readings but also *ourselves*" (957).

What Pinsker fails to account for as an essential part of the formative equation is himself. Though he presents his statements as universal truths, they are, in fact, autobiographical beliefs, intimately connected to his own reading experience. Pinsker's argument fails to account for an important point raised by Schriber in "Holden Caulfield, C'est Moi." Not everyone is "formed" by a formative book. Many readers respond to *Catcher* with far less passion, interest, and identification than Pinsker. Schriber notes, I think accurately, that *Catcher* is very much a boy's book and that the overwhelmingly androcentric criticism of the novel attests primarily (perhaps solely) to *male* experience (236). While Pinsker locates formativity "in the novel," positing the existence of "formative books," I believe we need to invert this equation and locate formativity in the reader. Rather than talking about formative books, we need to examine a "formative process"—an interaction where certain readers meet certain books in passionate and powerful ways.

Readerly Identification

In order to understand more fully what Pinsker and others mean by "falling in love" with a text, we need to return to the question of identification. Erikson and other psychologists have noted that one of the major problems with the term "identification" is that it suggests an interpsychic process (between two subjects), when, in fact, the phenomenon is better understood as an intrapsychic process: something that happens in the identifier's (for our purposes, the reader's) mind. This is not to suggest that the text has no role in the process of readerly identification but that its role is secondary, because the text must first be activated by a reader.

"Identification" means literally "making oneself the same as." When we identify with a person, we re-create some or all of their characteristics (or, more accurately, our vision of these characteristics—whether they be physical qualities, mannerisms, ideas, attitudes, or beliefs) in ourselves. In *The Dynamics of Literary Response*, Norman Holland argues that essentially the same process occurs with literary identifications:

> From the lines we are hearing, *we* recreate the characters, the words on the page controlling and shaping the characters we create. Then, in the writer's cliché, the characters "take on a life of their own," and in turn shape and inform the words on the page. (272)

The previous comments from writers who identified with Holden seem to bear out this description of identification as incorporation and recreation. Identifiers treat Holden not so much as a literary construct but as a person with "a life of his own" and, more importantly, as a person worthy of emulation. Christopher Parker indicates how enthusiastic young readers adopted what they perceived as Holden's central attitude ("It's also sort of a fad among us to be very critical of everything and everyone"), while Robert Gutwillig recalls the mirroring of Holden's manner of dress and speech ("[we] bought ourselves red caps with earflaps, and we all took to calling each other 'Ace' and 'Prince'"). Pinsker recalls similar forms of identification with Holden, such as in this example where the critic aligns his and Holden's world views:

> Like Holden, I yearned for a world more attractive, and less mutable, than the one in which we live and are forced to compete.... In those days Holden was my "secret sharer."...To be sure, what Holden said in bald print I dared only whisper *sotto voce*. (954, 956)

Pinsker suggests that he shares desires with Holden and that Holden, in fact, expresses these desires more aptly than he himself ever could. Holden becomes transformed into Pinsker's better self—a more clearly articulated version of who he could or should be. What the critic fails to recognize, however, is that his *sotto voce* whisperings are in fact what *make* Holden real for him. It is Pinsker's yearning that makes Holden's meaningful, not vice versa. This process is well summarized by Holland:

> The plot or incidents cause me [the reader] to have certain feelings or wishes or tensions. I feel these tensions from the play [or any text] as tensions in myself, but, both intellectually and emotionally, I attribute these tensions to the characters as motives: I project or bestow my feelings on the characters.... The more clearly a given character embodies my tensions, the more the work of art stimulates those tensions in me; the more I have those tensions in myself anyway—why, then, the more real a given character will seem. He will, ultimately, seem as real to me as I myself, for out of my own drives and needs for defense, I have created him. (274–5)

Like Pinsker's "secret sharer" who seems as real as the reader himself, those characters with whom we most identify take on a striking reality of their own. That Holden Caulfield has survived in such a dramatic way for five decades suggests that he is a creation who has stimulated a great degree of "tension" in a large number of readers.

For decades, reviewers and critics have been asking *why* so many people have identified with Holden. Perhaps a more relevant question is *what* so many readers have identified with. Following Holland, then, I propose to pursue an investigation of the tensions or feelings that the novel has caused in readers and which readers have projected back on Holden. If we can identify who or what readers think Holden is, we will also have discovered the main tensions or feelings that the novel has caused in the largest number of readers. I suggest that there are two stories that readers have continually told about Holden—the story of the sensitive outsider and of the boy who refused to grow up—and that these stories tell us as much about Holden's readers as they do about the character himself.

The image of Holden that has been most consistently drawn by readers in and out of academia is the picture of the "sensitive outsider." Repeatedly, Holden has been seen as the spokesman for disaffected youth, the outcast whose rebellion derives from his painful but lucid insights into the indifferent and "phony" adult world. It follows from the previous discussion that this construction of Holden is an important and often-repeated projection of his readers. Holden's alienation belongs equally to the fictional construct "Holden Caulfield" and to the multitude of readers who feel a similar affliction. *Catcher*'s initial popular success in the fifties (preceding its critical and academic canonization in the sixties) has much to do with young readers' identifications with the sensitive rebel. As Ian Hamilton explains:

> The so-called teenage revolution had begun in 1954, and by 1956 adolescent outsiderism was thoroughly established as a market force: Films like *The Wild One* and *Rebel Without a Cause* scored huge popular successes. Editorialists spoke darkly of a "youthquake." On university campuses Salinger's five-year-old novel had suddenly become the book all brooding adolescents had to buy, the indispensable manual from which cool styles of disaffection could be borrowed. *The Catcher in the Rye* was middle class and it gave voice to the malaise of the advantaged; it offered a college-boy version of Marlon Brando's leather jacket—a pacific, internalized manner of rebellion.... (155)

Although Hamilton is certainly not the first to suggest this, I think he is essentially correct in characterizing Holden's as a safe, middle-class rebellion.[3] Holden's chauffeured odyssey from an expensive prep school to a private Californian clinic, stopping along the way at nightclubs, hotels, theaters, museums, skating rinks, and his family's distinctly upper-middle-class apartment, may be one of an outsider—but this is clearly a privileged outsider. It is probably the safety and ease of Holden's rebellion that made it so attractive, and so identifiable, to many young (and not so young) readers. Pinsker notes correctly that *Catcher* "has always had more appeal to rebels under the skin than to those who actually lugged their failing transcripts from one prep school to another" (959).

As so many commentators make clear, Holden was embraced by a certain, predominantly male (though not necessarily all adolescent) part of the culture as a character who spoke to their own feelings of alienation. Bernard Kinnick's comments help reveal the values attached to the rebellion Holden was made to represent:

> Many adults feel that the adolescent (characterized here by Holden Caulfield) should "grow up," accept the world for what it is, and live in it.... But, is it not possible that there are some adolescents (and adults) who are simply not like the majority, who cannot accept the human condition for what it is, who cannot resign themselves to the existence of injustice, ugliness, and pain?...These individuals wage war with the-way-things-are. They are the martyrs in the eternal search for idealism. Holden Caulfield, if he is a rebel at all, is a rebel against the human condition and as such he deserves his small share of nobility. (31)

Kinnick's overstated rhetoric makes several things clear. Firstly, Kinnick is not only talking about Holden but also about himself (he places himself, with no great subtlety, in the parenthetical "and adults" aside). Kinnick commends Holden's non-conformity as a way of validating his own. Holden's refusal to "grow up" becomes a mirror of Kinnick's own refusal to abandon youthful idealism. Holden flatters those readers who imagine themselves, *like Holden*, as "martyrs...simply not like the majority ...unwilling to accept the world for what it is." The outsider, after all, is an outcast because of his special gift, his insight, and his inability to accept "the-way-things-are." Identifying with Holden becomes a way for "rebels under the skin" to validate their own silent rebellion. Valorizing Holden becomes a way of metaphorically entering a special club of sensitive outsiders; it is a way of distinguishing "us" (those like Holden) from "them" (the "phonies" of Holden's world, or the "adults" of Kinnick's). By recognizing Holden's giftedness or superiority, readers are aided in constructing their own.

We are beginning to develop a picture of both how and why readers found value in identifying themselves with Holden as sensitive outsider. As suggested previously, though, it was not only young, "unsophisticated" readers who saw Holden in this light. As Salinger and Holden were incorporated into the academy in the sixties, the boundaries of the sensitive outsider discourse were greatly expanded as academics embraced the troubled young protagonist as one of their own. The movement of Salinger from the ranks of the student ghetto into the halls of the academy can be easily traced. Gutwillig has already noted the sudden and remarkable adoption of *Catcher* by colleges and universities in the early sixties. As another indication, Hamilton notes that between 1951 and 1956 only three articles (apart from book reviews) appeared on Salinger; whereas between 1956 and 1960, more than seventy articles on *Catcher* alone appeared in British and American magazines (156). Many of these articles presented what would have been a familiar, though now more fully articulated, picture of the sensitive outsider. Throughout the fifties and sixties we find essays and book chapters in which Holden is variously described as "The Misfit Hero" (Paul Levine, 1958), the "Alien in the Rye" (Albert Fowler, 1957), the "Good Bad Boy" (Leslie Fiedler, 1958), "The Responsive Outsider" or "rebel-victim" (Ihab Hassan, 1961), and the "Absurd Hero" (David Galloway, 1966). It is probably unsurprising that not only adolescents and college students but also those people employed to instruct these students found value and interest in portraying Holden as sensitive outsider. If students found a hero and role model in a character who "challenged the system" while essentially remaining in safe complicity with that system, what better hero was there for their instructors to embrace?

Surveying some of these early *Catcher* articles, we find a growing discourse around a familiar theme. The first substantial critical article, Heiserman and Miller's "J. D. Salinger: Some Crazy Cliff," established a much-repeated pattern by placing Holden in a long continuum of outcast heroes "who def[y] traditions in order to arrive at some pristine knowledge, some personal integrity" (32). Where his younger readership valorized Holden by making him into a cultural icon, a James Dean or Marlon Brando in a red hunting cap, his more sophisticated readers valorized him in essentially the same way: by associating him with their iconic literary heroes. "He is Stephen Dedalus and Leopold Bloom rolled into one crazy kid," write Heiserman and Miller (33).

Articles from the fifties and sixties compared Holden to everyone from Huck Finn to Jesus Christ. Essays such as Ihab Hassan's "J. D. Salinger: Rare Quixotic Gesture," and Jonathan Baumbach's "The Saint as a Young Man: A Reappraisal of *The Catcher in the Rye*" did not so much reappraise the novel as extend the myth of Holden, envisioning him as a kind of secular saint. Valorizing Holden provided a neat package of both self-promotion and self-justification. On the promotional side, these articles were apparently quite salable—everyone wanted to read about Holden; why not give the people what they wanted? And what better method of promotion for these young academics than to find brilliance exactly where their students wanted them to find it? At the same time, these articles were self-justifying. They were elevating a rebellion in complicity that was probably not far from home for the rebellious young academics of the sixties, who were no doubt young readers of *Catcher* in the fifties and who needed to justify their own complicity in a "phony" educational system that Holden (as well as other Salinger counterparts like Franny, Seymour, or Buddy Glass) held in such contempt. Commending Holden's outsiderism was a way of tacitly participating in it. Pinsker, for example, celebrates *Catcher*'s opening line—in which Holden refers to his autobiography as "that David Copperfield kind of crap"—in the following manner:

> To call a Dickens novel crap—and in the same sentence that heaves in a "lousy" no less!—was to yank literature away from those who pronounced it "lit-er-ah-tour." (956)

Pinsker's excitement suggests that he imagines Salinger's or Holden's project (the "yanking" of literature away from pedants with fake British accents) to be one with his own. Once again, the reader's own desires (in this case the iconoclastic yearnings of the rebel-professor) are projected onto the character.

The creation and discussion of the sensitive outsider fulfilled a number of important functions for both amateur and professional readers. Holden not only stood for and validated their own silent rebellion, but he made that rebellion easy and safe, for finally Holden's sedition was one that could be worked on in the privacy of their own homes or the comfort of an English classroom. Holden allowed readers to vicariously participate in the thrill of his loudly announced, though only momentarily lived, marginalization.[4]

A modification and extension of the sensitive outsider figure is suggested by Henry Grunwald, who calls Holden "A Beatnik Peter Pan." Many readers saw Holden's rebellion as intimately connected with his refusal to "grow up" (in Kinnick's words). In his tenacious devotion to the "idealism of adolescence" (Kinnick 31), Holden became, for some, a wistful Peter Pan-like rebel. Hence, *Catcher* was read, in the words of John Aldridge, as a "study in the spiritual picaresque, the journey that for the young is all one way, from holy innocence to such knowledge as the world offers" (50). For many young readers, as for Holden himself, what the world seemed to offer was nothing but phoniness, greed, and the hypocrisy of adults like Holden's history teacher, Mr. Spencer, who insist that "Life is a game." In opposition to the cynical and depressing facts of the adult world, readers installed Holden as the chosen spokesman for what Leslie Fiedler calls "the Cult of the Child" (Grunwald 242).

Once again, Heiserman and Miller's article sets the tone for succeeding Peter Pan readings. As with their comments on Holden as outsider, the critics once again validate him by placing Holden's story in a continuum of "great works":

> Childhood and the loss of innocence have obsessed much of western literature at least since the Enlightenment.... Emile, Candide, the young Wordsworth, Huck Finn, Holden Caulfield—all lament or seek a return to a lost childhood.... But it is Holden's tragedy that he is sixteen, and like Wordsworth he can never be less. (34–35)

Although Holden may be sixteen, he often acts (in his own words) "like I was only about twelve"—in other words, as a child. As Heiserman and Miller (and others) have noted, most of the signs of value which accumulate around Holden are images suggestive of childhood. Holden's penchant for "horsing around"; his attachment to all children (particularly Phoebe and the eternal child, Allie) and to "childish" things (the ducks, the hunting cap, the pieces of a broken record, or a cherished snowball); his sexual naiveté and apprehension; and of course his *Catcher* fantasy of saving the children before they fall off that crazy cliff into adulthood—all these, and many more images in the novel, were read as signs of Holden's special connection to the unspoiled world of the child.

To many, Holden's devotion to childhood was much more than just a rebellion against "phony adultism" (Heiserman and Miller 39), it became a symbol of spontaneity, idealism, and naive goodness. Holden's reluctance to "grow up" was seen not a case of immaturity but in fact the inverse: a sign of his gifted, superior intelligence and sensitivity. "Holden is not rejecting maturity," writes Granville Hicks, "but is looking for a better model than his elders by and large. Like the Glasses, though in a less ostentatious way, he is a seeker after wisdom" (214). Heiserman and Miller make an even stronger case for Holden's naiveté, seeing it as the only true "health" in the midst of "sickness":

> It is not Holden who should be examined for a sickness of the mind, but the world in which he has sojourned and found himself alien. To "cure" Holden, he must be given the contagious, almost universal disease of phony adultism; he must be pushed over that "crazy cliff." (39)

As in the previous case of sensitive outsider criticism, I believe that the Peter Pan interpretations were attractive and useful because they were self-validating. Once again, readers found in Holden those qualities which they admired most in themselves. The construction of Holden as a visionary Peter Pan has one important similarity with the figuration of the sensitive outsider: both indicate a kind of superiority. Whether this superiority is seen as intellectual, moral, or emotional, its construction is once again based on an "us" versus "them" dichotomy. Holden and those readers who identify with him become part of a fraternity of gifted children. And once again, membership in this fraternity is defined predominantly through opposition with the "phonies" of the "adult" world. [5] Grunwald highlights the appeal of youth and the past when he suggests that "In cherishing the child we cherish ourselves, or rather, the memory of ourselves in youth. We hug what we once were, or think we were" (xvii). If we replace the word "child" with "Holden," I believe we have a fairly accurate reading of why so many people have "cherished" Holden Caulfield.

Since Holden is almost always first encountered by readers in their adolescence and because his story is the familiar one about a perennial attachment to adolescence, it is not surprising that Holden has become, for so many, the quintessential adolescent. Likewise, it should not be surprising that Holden has often been used by readers as a way of returning to their own adolescence. Holden's experiences and emotions, conflicts and excitements act as a trigger to re-animate similar feelings in receptive readers. To a great extent, these feelings follow classical patterns of adolescent "identity crisis" as described by Erik Erikson in *Identity: Youth and Crisis*. Erikson's research on adolescent and young adult behavior highlights a number of characteristics that seem highly applicable to Holden.

In Erikson's general scheme of psycho-social development, Holden is in the fifth (adolescent and young adult) stage which is marked by the problem of identity. According to Erikson, this is the time of life in which individuals begin seriously asking the question "who am I?" Adolescence is a period marked by conflicts, tensions, excitements, distortions, and the general anxiety of such personal exploration. Many of these anxieties are noted by Holden and highlighted by Holden's explicators. For example, adolescents are often ambivalent or hostile towards parents and authority figures, a trait clearly portrayed by Holden. According to Erikson, authority figures are often transformed into "negative identities" who represent everything the young person does *not* want to be. A important part of *Catcher*'s structure and appeal revolves around such negativity, as Holden illustrates when he mutters, "Game my ass" (to himself and to his young confidant, the reader) when his teacher suggests that life is a game. Furthermore, an Eriksonian analysis would connect Holden's formation of negative identities with his penchant for dropping out or running away. Whether dropping out of school, planning to move "out West," or fantasizing about leaving behind the whole phony business of verbal communication, Holden's desires amount to the same thing according to Erikson:

> Youth after youth, bewildered by the incapacity to assume a role forced on him by the inexorable standardization of American adolescence, runs away in one form or another, dropping out of school, leaving jobs, staying out all night, or withdrawing into bizarre and inaccessible moods. (132)

Holden becomes a mirror for many readers in this regard. The dynamics of identification here are well summarized by Erikson's concept of moratorium:

> A moratorium is a period of delay granted to somebody who is not ready to meet an obligation or forced on somebody who should give himself time. By psychosocial moratorium, then, we mean a delay of adult commitments, and yet it is not only a delay. It is a period that is characterized by selective permissiveness on the part of society and provocative playfulness on the part of youth, and yet it also often leads to deep, if often transitory, commitment on the part of youth.... (157)

Holden's refusal to "grow up" marks a vital moment in the maturity process, according to Erikson (156). Though undoubtedly a time of confusion, the moratorium period is also one of great freedom. It is a time of adventurous exploration, filled with a romantic sense of either unattachment or profound but transitory attachment. Holden's adventures in New York may be marked by depression, confusion, and loneliness, but the pleasure that many readers take in them comes from the sense of unencumbered, playful excitement. It is this sense that made the "Beatnik Peter Pan" so attractive to so many readers.

Schriber's "Holden Caulfield, C'est Moi" introduces some of the questions about identification that I have tried to expand upon here:

> The essential ingredient in the phenomenal success and the critical reception of *The Catcher in the Rye* is the propensity of critics to identify with Salinger's protagonist. Holden Caulfield, c'est moi. Falling in love with him as with their very selves, they fall in love with the novel as well. (227)

What Schriber does not ask is with *whom* these critics fall in love. In other words, whom do they imagine Holden (and by extension, themselves) to be? I have suggested two main identifying stories: Holden the sensitive outsider and Holden the perennial adolescent, which account for critical acts which simultaneously valorize Holden and validate their authors. Rather than talking about formative *books*, which compel readers to change their lives, it may be more accurate and useful to talk about a formative *response*, a complicated, messy, and sometimes volatile interaction that occurs between text and reader. With Salinger's novel these responses have ranged from the tame criticism of a Heiserman, Miller, or Pinsker to the more irrational expressions of a fan(atic) like Mark David Chapman, who, like Lennon's visitor in the opening of this essay, felt compelled by a particular work of art. That the author of one novel and several dozen stories has seized and compelled our collective imagination for so long is testament as much to our need for the kind of story he tells as it is to Salinger's undeniable talent for providing this story.

NOTES

1. To the best of my knowledge, only one of three potential books that Davidson mentions as forthcoming from panelists Dennis L. O'Connor, James P. Doyle, and Eberhard Alsen was ever published. Alsen's monograph, *Salinger's Glass Stories as a Composite Novel*, was published by Whitson in 1983.

2. The MLA index lists no fewer than thirty items on Salinger written in Japanese.

3. Hamilton is certainly not the first to make this point. As early as 1958, Maxwell Geismar commented on Holden's "Ivy League Rebellion" in this way: "This is surely the differential revolt of the lonesome rich child, the conspicuous display of leisure-class emotions, the wounded affections, never quite faced, of the upper-class orphan" (Laser and Fruman 76).

4. It is worth noting that Salinger's later creations, Franny and Buddy Glass, exhibit the same kind of safe, complicitous rebellion. Franny loudly challenges the pretensions and absurdities of college as she gets her degree from one, while Buddy tears down the critical and teaching establishments in which he continues to work.

5. This Salinger "fraternity" becomes far more literalized in the later Glass stories. Here readers are invited to become honorary members of the visionary Glass family. These stories are full of gestures which invite readers into an intimate, almost familial relationship with the characters. Readers are constantly shown private letters, notes, and diaries; they are subjected at length to Buddy Glass's "prose home movies." All of these intimate encounters are presented in "an esoteric family language," which is (according to narrator Buddy Glass) "a sort of semantic geometry in which the shortest distance between any two points is a fullish circle" (*Franny and Zooey* 49).

WORKS CITED

Aldridge, John W. *In Search of Heresy: American Literature in an Age of Conformity*. Expt. in Laser and Fruman 50–52.

Alley, Alvin D. "Puritanism: Scourge of Education Today?" *Clearing House* 38: 7 (1964): 394–395. Rpt. in Bloom 16–17.

Baumbach, Jonathan. "The Saint as a Young Man: A Reappraisal of *The Catcher in the Rye*." Salzberg 55–66.

Bloom, Harold, ed. *Holden Caulfield*. Major Literary Characters Series. New York: Chelsea House, 1990.

Burger, Nash K. "Books of *The Times*." *New York Times*, 16 July 1951: 19.

Davidson, Richard Allan. "Salinger Criticism and 'The Laughing Man': A Case of Arrested Development." *Studies in Short Fiction* 18:1 (1981): 1–15.

Engle, Paul. "Honest Tale of Distraught Adolescent." *Chicago Sunday Tribune Magazine of Books*, 15 July 1951: 3.

Erikson, Erik H. *Identity: Youth and Crisis*. New York: Norton, 1968.

Fiedler, Leslie A. "The Eye of Innocence." Grunwald 241–71.

Fowler, Albert. "Alien in the Rye." Belcher and Lee 34–40.

Galloway, David D. *The Absurd Hero in American Fiction: Updike, Styron, Bellow, Salinger*. Austin: U of Texas P, 1966.

Goodman, Anne L. "Mad About Children." *New Republic* 125 (1951): 20–21. Rpt. in Salzberg 23–24.

Grunwald, Henry Anatole, ed. *Salinger: A Critical and Personal Portrait*. New York: Pocket Books, 1963.

Gutwillig, Robert. "Everybody's Caught *The Catcher in the Rye*." Laser and Fruman 1–6.

Hamilton, Ian. *In Search of J. D. Salinger*. New York: Random House, 1988.

Hassan, Ihab. "J. D. Salinger: The Rare Quixotic Gesture." Grunwald 150–79.

———. "The Victim: Images of Evil in Recent American Fiction." *College English* 21 (1959): 140–146.

Heiserman, Arthur, and James E. Miller, Jr. "J. D. Salinger: Some Crazy Cliff." Salzberg 32–39.

Hicks, Granville. "The Search for Wisdom." Grunwald 211–214.

Holland, Norman. *The Dynamics of Literary Response*. New York: Oxford UP, 1968.

Imagine: John Lennon, the Definitive Film Portrait. Dir. Andrew Solt. Narrated by John Lennon. Warner Bros., 1988.

Jones, Ernest. "Case History of All of Us." *The Nation* 173: 9 (1951): 176. Rpt. in Salzberg 24–25.

Kinnick, Bernard C. "Holden Caulfield: Adolescents' Enduring Model." *High School Journal* 53: 8 (1970): 440–443. Rpt. in Bloom 30–32.

Laser, Martin, and Norman Fruman, eds. *Studies in J.D. Salinger: Reviews, Essays, and Critiques of* The Catcher in the Rye *and Other Fiction.* New York: Odyssey Press, 1963.

Levine, Paul. "J. D. Salinger: The Development of the Misfit Hero." Belcher and Lee 107–115.

Longstreth, Morris T. Rev. of *The Catcher in the Rye. Christian Science Monitor,* 19 July 1951: 11. Rpt. in Salzberg 30–31.

Miller, Jr. James E. *J. D. Salinger.* Minneapolis: U of Minnesota Press, 1965: 5, 8. Rpt. in Bloom 20.

Parker, Christopher. "Why the Hell *Not* Smash All the Windows?" Grunwald 280–85.

Pinsker, Sanford. *"The Catcher in the Rye* and All: Is the Age of Formative Books Over?" *The Georgia Review* 50: 4 (1986): 953–967.

Ralston, Nancy C. "Holden Caulfield: Super-Adolescent." *Adolescence* 24 (1971): 429–432. Rpt. in Bloom 32–34.

Rodriquez, J. S. "Youth—American Style." *Montreal Gazette,* 22 September 1951: 25.

Romano, John. "Salinger Was Playing Our Song." *New York Times Book Review,* 3 June 1979: 10–13.

Salinger, J. D. *The Catcher in the Rye.* New York: Bantam, 1964.

———. *Franny and Zooey.* Boston: Little, 1961.

Salzberg, Joel, ed. *Critical Essays on Salinger's* The Catcher in the Rye. Critical Essays on American Literature. Boston: G.K. Hall, 1990.

Salzman, Jack, ed. Introduction. *New Essays on* The Catcher in the Rye. Cambridge: Cambridge UP, 1991.

Schriber, Mary Suzanne. "Holden Caulfield, C'est Moi." Salzberg 226–238.

Steiner, George. "The Salinger Industry." Laser and Fruman 113–119.

Sublette, Jack R. *J.D. Salinger: An Annotated Bibliography, 1938–81*. New York: Garland Publishing, 1984.

2.

Mentor Mori; or,
Sibling Society and the *Catcher* in the Bly

ROBERT MILTNER

Holden Caulfield is a young man coming of age in American society in the 1950s; caught in the adolescent transition between the childhood of his past and the adulthood which awaits him, he struggles in an uncertainty which seems as prolonged as adolescence itself, against "the ineluctability of growing up, of having to assume the prerogatives and responsibilities of manhood" (55) as Jonathan Baumbach puts it. What makes Holden's experience particularly difficult is that he is keenly aware of being isolated and feeling alienated; seemingly, there is no one he can turn to for guidance, as those few he does turn to do not provide him with effective help. Possible elder mentors—his father, his brother D. B., his former teacher Mr. Antolini, even his former student advisor Carl Luce—are unavailable or, when contacted, have other agendas, while his prep school peers—Stradlater, Ackley, James Castle—offer versions of Holden's future from which he recoils. No wonder, then, that Holden reveres the time of his own childhood, represented by his little sister Phoebe and his deceased younger brother Allie, who remains frozen at the threshold of adolescence. No wonder then that the image which mirrors Holden most closely, the Holden who fears stepping off the curb for fear of disappearing, is the image of the "swell" kid who walks in the street next to the curb singing "If a body catch a body coming through the rye" (*Catcher in the Rye* 115).

Initial critical response in the 1950s identified Holden as being a poor role model, as in Riley Hughes' dismissal of Holden for his "formidably excessive use of amateur swearing and coarse language"(8) or in T. Morris Longstreth's alliterative pronouncement that Holden was "preposterous, profane, and pathetic beyond belief" (6). From a contemporary perspective, however, it is evident that part of Holden's difficulty arises not so much from Holden being a poor role model as much as his having no one after which to model himself. Suspended between the world of prep schools and an upper-middle-class New York lifestyle, between childhood and adulthood, Holden is adrift in a sea of peers every bit as adrift as he is. In essence, Holden's 1950s dilemma foreshadows the sibling society of the late 1990s and early 2000s.

Robert Bly has identified a sibling society as one in which adults, due to single-parenting and divorce, fueled by the media-driven emphasis on the youth culture, are less mature and responsible than their parent's generation. Conversely, and more importantly, adolescents, due to growing up in working, single-parent homes, assume more adult responsibilities; the sibling society is thus one in which "parents regress to become more like children, and the children, through abandonment, are forced to become adults too soon" (Bly *Sibling Society* 132). The result is a society in which adults and adolescent are becoming less differentiated. This problem is further complicated as people remain adolescents long past the normal adolescent period (*Sibling Society* 45). Historically, as Bly recounts, social conditions did not allow for adolescence:

> During the Middle Ages, the stage of youth was virtually ignored; a peasant child of seven joined the workforce. At Plymouth Colony, a child was considered a small adult at the age of eight. Children were asked to be aware of the group. There was no real time for adolescence then. (*Sibling Society* 45)

Not until the late 1940s and early 1950s, the era of *The Catcher in the Rye*, did adolescence became both a social presence and a cultural concept, as linguist Bill Bryson illustrates:

> So little had they [adolescents] been noticed in the past that *teenager* had entered the language only as recently as 1941. (As an adjective, *teenage* had been around since the 1920s, but it wasn't used much.) In the heady boom of the postwar years, however, America's teenagers made up for lost time. Between 1946 and 1960, when the population of the United States grew by about 40 percent, the number of teenagers grew by 110 percent. (335)

It is evident, then, that Holden's generation represents the beginning of periodic social trends in which adolescents would outnumber adults. Holden Caulfield, in his disdain for the phoniness of joining cliques and climbing the ladder of economic success, presages the emergence of the sibling society which dominates the cultural landscape of the 1960s and beyond: in lieu of accepting the cultural norm, they learn that "one way to outwit the demands of that civilization [their parent's] is to set up a sibling society" (*Sibling Society* 48). Yet, in accepting peer guidance from a society of siblings, young men come of age without the guidance of effective male role models, which Bly considers to be the basic problem the whole sibling society faces: "the socialization of young males in the absence of fathers and mentors" (*Sibling Society* 180). In the paternal society, the world of the first half of the twentieth century, there were numerous representatives of the adult community, teachers, and elders to whom the young were drawn (*Sibling Society* 237). These elders are necessary for modeling, a socialization process intrinsic to adolescence that allows young people to imitate elders and role models until their acquired responses become habitual. Among the elders, parents are the "most significant adults in the lives of adolescents," followed by siblings and non-related significant adults, such as teachers (Rice 96). In Holden's case, this applies especially to his father.

Holden's father, a corporate lawyer, is largely absent from the book, though his comings and goings are made evident. At best a "shadowy abstraction" (Rowe 89), Mr. Caulfield is described doing such mundane activities as driving the family car to a party in Norwalk, Connecticut (*Catcher in the Rye* 162–3), and flying to California for business (162), and he is even described sympathetically as lunching with Mr. Antolini to discuss how he is "terribly concerned" about Holden (186), yet he is never shown actually interacting with Holden in any way. Presented as an absentee parent, he is typical of "many contemporary fathers [who] abandon the family emotionally by working fourteen hours a day" (*Sibling Society* 36), and is representative of Bly's belief that fathers are vanishing both physically and conceptually in the sibling society. Holden's father is presented as a private person given to strong emotional responses, as early as the first paragraph in which Holden expresses that both of his parents are "quite touchy" about discussing "anything pretty personal about them," and Holden adds "especially my father" (*Catcher in the Rye* 1) to emphasize that his father is the more emphatic of the two. When Phoebe learns that Holden has been dismissed from Pency Prep, she says, and repeats three more times for emphasis, that their Daddy will kill Holden for getting kicked out of school. However, Holden's father, who could not convince his son to be psychoanalyzed when Allie died, threatens Holden with the trump card in learning self-discipline: sending Holden to military school (166), that 1950s version of juvenile delinquent boot camp for an attitude readjustment. Holden's father is an example of the typical "Fifties male" Robert Bly examines in *Iron John*, one who "got to work early, labored responsibly, supported his wife and children, and admired discipline" (1), a type the generation into which Salinger and Bly were born in 1919 and 1926, respectively, knew well. Yet rather than be angry with or disdainful of his father, Holden seems largely ambivalent not only about his father but about the adult world in general.

Holden's mother, the other parental figure, is described as distant, distracted; she is, as Joyce Rowe observes, "too nervous and anxious herself to do more than pay perfunctory attention to her children's needs" (89). Holden expresses that she is "*nice* and all" (*Catcher in the Rye* 1) and that he feels "sorry as hell" for her because he is aware that her grief has not ended, since she "still isn't over [his] brother Allie yet" (155). The result of her continued grief leaves her "very nervous" (107), suffering from "headaches quite frequently" (178), and experiencing symptoms akin to agoraphobia: she "doesn't enjoy herself much when she goes out" (177), and despite her telling Phoebe she "won't be home until very late" (162), she returns early. This latter incident results in Holden's being caught off guard and having to hide in Phoebe's (D. B.'s) closet, and consequently Holden's mother appears only as a ghostly presence speaking from the dark, a figure which Holden can hear but not see. Concerning this absence of parental role models in the novel, Gerald Rosen has commented that

The absence of Holden's parents (along with the absence of real religious guidance in the form of a school chaplain or family minister) is so important it amounts to a presence…. Holden sorely misses being able to turn to his parents in his time of trouble…. So Holden cannot get advice on how to leave the world of childhood from the adults around him. (162)

Because Holden's parents are unable to assist him during his transition through adolescence, his next best choice is D. B., his older brother.

D. B., however, has deserted Holden, abandoning his true artistry as a short story writer to go to Hollywood and to write for the movies, which leads Holden to label his brother a "prostitute" (*Catcher in the Rye* 2). As a middle child—both the middle boy and, after Allie's death, the middle Caulfield child—Holden looks up to his older brother who has served in the Army and who has written and published a book that Holden admires. It was D. B. who functioned as Holden's surrogate by attending Allie's funeral when Holden was still in the hospital from hurting his hand by breaking the garage windows the night Allie died, and it is through D. B.'s eyes—"D. B. told me. I wasn't there" (155)— that Holden waked his little brother. Sibling relationships between older brothers who act as role models and younger siblings who imitate them can be "vitally important" (Rice 441) in the development of an adolescent's personality traits and overall behavior. Further, these older siblings often serve "as surrogate parents, acting as caretakers, teachers, playmates and confidants" (Rice 441), a concept not unfamiliar to Salinger who presented older siblings as surrogate parents in *Franny and Zooey* as well. Buddy Glass, for example, in a letter to his younger brother Zooey, describes how he and his brother Seymour took over the education of the two youngest Glass children, Franny and Zooey, remarking how "Seymour and I thought it might be a good thing to hold back" the usual areas of conventional knowledge, such as "the arts, sciences, classics, languages"(*Franny and Zooey* 65); instead, he reminds Zooey of how "[Seymour] and I were regularly conducting home seminars" on "who and what Jesus and Gautama and Lao-tse . . . were before you knew too much or anything about Homer or Shakespeare or even Blake or Whitman, let alone George Washington and his cherry tree"

(65–66). Yet, following Seymour's suicide and Buddy's relocation—similar to Allie's death and D. B.'s relocation, respectively—Franny and Zooey find themselves mentorless with absentee older siblings. Similarly, after Allie's death, D. B. relocates to Hollywood, making himself "as emotionally remote from him [Holden] as is his father" (Rowe 89). As a result, Holden feels betrayed, partly because D. B. has become a scriptwriter for money rather than an artist who writes stories and partly because it connects D. B. to the commercial world of his father, who flies to California for business of his own. Holden is left to seek other mentors who can function as surrogate older brothers or as surrogate parents.

The person to whom Holden turns is Mr. Antolini, his former teacher from Elkton Hills who now teaches English at NYU. It is noteworthy that Antolini, like Holden, has read all of D. B.'s stories and further that he has "phoned [D. B.] up and told him not to go [to Hollywood]" (*Catcher in the Rye* 181), so that Antolini speaks like an older version of Holden, telling D. B. what Holden is feeling but cannot express. Further, and despite Holden's being drawn to Mr. Antolini because he was the "best teacher I [Holden] ever had" or because "you could kid around with him without losing your respect for him" (174), that is, he could be both a child and an adult simultaneously, what is most telling about Holden's interest in his connection with Mr. Antolini is that "He was a pretty young guy, not much older than my brother D. B." (174), and Holden even asserts that Antolini was "sort of like D. B." (181). Clearly, then, with D. B. away, Antolini becomes a surrogate older brother, someone his brother's age with whom Holden can talk. In fact, just following Holden's sharing of his vision of the catcher in the rye with Phoebe, his only local living sibling, his immediate instinct is to call Antolini, his surrogate brother. Despite his inability to call Jane Gallagher when he needed to do so, Holden calls Antolini and arranges to visit with him, going quickly by cab from D. B.'s room where Phoebe sleeps to Antolini's apartment where he is greeted intimately and familially as "Holden, m'boy!" (181). Thus Antolini, the "gentle teacher— the substitute father," is the one Holden turns to "after all the other fathers of his world have failed him, including his real father" (Baumbach 56). Yet,

Antolini fails him in his own way as familialism becomes unwelcome homosexual intimacy, and Holden's father figure and surrogate older brother joins the league of disappointing older males; if D. B. is the "prostitute," then Antolini is the gigolo. Which makes Carl Luce the sex counselor.

Like Antolini, Carl Luce represents a mentor brought forward from Holden's previous prep school experiences to function as a surrogate older brother, except where Antolini represents Holden's experiences at Elkton Hills, Luce represents Holden's experiences at Whooton School. Further, like Antolini, Luce has left the prep school (he has graduated) and gone on to college (as a student) at Columbia. Three years older than Holden, Carl Luce was Holden's Student Advisor at Whooton, a kind of peer-mentoring position, though in reality

> the only thing he [Luce] ever did, though, was give these sex talks and all, late at night when there was a bunch of guys in his room. He knew quite a bit about sex, especially perverts and all. (*Catcher in the Rye* 143)

In a sense, Carl Luce plays the role usually reserved for one's father or one's older brother: initiation, through talk and male bonding, into understanding the world of sexuality, an area in which Holden is floundering due to his lack of experience. Holden, recognizing that he is in need of a mentor to guide him, meets Carl Luce at the Wicker Bar, only to have his request to be guided rejected. Holden asks Luce to listen, praises his intelligence, then states in no uncertain terms that he is in need of Luce's advice, but before he can state the nature of his problem, Carl Luce cuts him off with a dismissive groan. Carl Luce has no interest in mentoring Holden; he refuses to answer any typical Caulfield questions (146) or have a typical Caulfield conversation (145), premised, apparently, upon his belief that Holden is not old enough or mature enough to benefit from his advice even should he give it, as evidenced by his asking Holden repeatedly about when he's going to grow up (144–46). Luce acts like the older brother who feels his younger brother is just too little to be talked to as a adult, a role, by the way, which Holden never plays with either Allie (in his imagined conversations) or Phoebe. And what's worse, Carl Luce's attempt to act older than his years, manifest in his dating a Chinese sculptress in her late thirties, is similar to Mr. Antolini's being married to a wife who is, from Holden's perspective, "about sixty years older" (181). This is the same "older woman" stratagem, by the way, which Holden himself parallels by offering to buy drinks for Ernie Morrow's mother (57), Faith Cavendish (65), the three secretaries from Seattle (74), and the Hat Check Girl at the Wicker Bar (153). Additionally, Carl Luce, again like Antolini, sides with the absent Mr. Caulfield; where Antolini met Holden's father for lunch (a kind of power lunch in Holden's interest), Luce sides with Holden's father in believing that Holden needs to be psychoanalyzed (148). Luce allays Holden's concerns about psychiatry, advising him that it will help him to "recognize the patterns of [his] mind" (148), but just as Carl Luce begins to explain the concept to Holden, to actually mentor him—an extension upon his previous role as a student advisor—he suddenly changes tack, stops, and retreats: "Listen. I'm not giving an elementary course in psychoanalysis. If you're interested, call him [Luce's father] up and make an appointment" (148). Despite Luce's directive for Holden to call his father, however, Luce's personal comment is more telling: "If you're not [interested], don't. I couldn't care less, frankly" (148). Carl Luce clearly indicates that he has no personal interest in guiding or mentoring Holden; in fact, while Holden is ironically telling Luce, hand on his shoulder, what a "real friendly bastard" he is, Luce is looking at his watch and calling to the bartender for his check (148). Of course, when Carl Luce tells Holden how he was psychoanalyzed and was able, in his words, able "to ad*just* [him]self to a certain extent" (148), it is becoming clear to Holden that if psychoanalysis will leave him as distant and disinterested as Carl Luce—and his own father by proxy—then he will not be seeking out a psychiatrist. Carl Luce leaves Holden at the bar, alone, without the benefit of any mentoring or guidance.

In a world devoid, therefore, of older male role models, either father figures or older brother surrogates, Holden is left with the peer group, his sibling society, represented by the prep schools which Holden has attended:

Whooton School, Elkton Hills, and Pency Prep. At Whooton School, Holden's peers include Raymond Goldfarb, with whom Holden drank Scotch in the chapel (*Catcher in the Rye* 90), in what appears to be an initiation into the adult alcohol culture which attracts Holden. He finds his other peers, Quaker Arthur Childs (99) and Catholic Louis Shaney (112), want to foist their religious agendas on him. Thus, Whooton School teaches Holden that consumption of alcohol and religious affiliation are signifiers of the adult world, with Holden choosing the former. At Elkton Hills, Holden's peers teach him more personal lessons. One of his roommates, Dick Slagle, had a "goddam inferiority complex" (108) because his inexpensive suitcases were not "Mark Cross . . . genuine cowhide" (108) like Holden's; as a result, Slagle labels Holden's suitcases "too new and bourgeois" (108), giving Holden a lesson in class distinction (the visual signifier of the object-suitcase) and class jealousy (suitcases connote both where one comes from as well as where one is going), which Holden summarizes in his observation that:

> You think if they're [roommate/peer] intelligent and all, the other person, and have a good sense of humor, that they don't give a damn whose suitcases are better, but they do. They really do. (109)

His other roommate, Harris Macklin, whistles beautifully but is "one of the biggest bores [Holden] ever met" (123). Here the talent, whistling, is offset by the personality deficiency of being boring. The lesson Holden learns is summed up in Holden's comment on bores:

> Maybe you shouldn't feel too sorry if you see some swell girl getting married to [a bore]. They don't hurt anybody, most of them, and maybe they're secretly terrific whistlers or something. (124)

Hinted at, both by extension and by contrast, is that Jane Gallagher would be better off with a bore for a stepfather than the "booze hound" (78) Mr. Cudahy with the "lousy personality" who Holden worries might be trying to "get wise" (79) with Jane.

Perhaps the peer who taught Holden the greatest lesson at Elkton Hills was James Castle, who committed suicide by jumping from a window after refusing to take back his statement about how conceited James Stabile was. Castle functions as a emblem for integrity and truth and exemplifies the price paid by those who adhere to those principles: Castle spoke his mind, would not retract, and, instead of taking back what he said, jumped out the dorm window to his death (170). Several ironies are evident here. First, Holden, at numerous times during the novel, considers suicide in similar ways: once, when thinking about Stradlater with Jane Gallagher in Ed Banky's car, Holden comments "I felt like jumping out the window" (48), and second, after Maurice punches him, Holden stated that he felt like "jumping out the window" (104), a statement he expands upon by adding that "I probably would've done it, too, if I'd been sure somebody'd cover me up as soon as I landed. I didn't want a bunch of stupid rubbernecks looking at me when I was all gory" (104). This comment which ends chapter 14 is interesting, because it is not until chapter 22 that Holden identifies himself as one of the rubbernecks looking at James Castle when he was gory as "his teeth, and blood, were all over the place" (170)—and echoing the image Holden sees in the mirror after Stradlater hit him, "You never saw such gore in your life. I had blood all over my mouth and chin" (45)— followed by the revelation in the next chapter that it was Antolini who "took off his coat and put it over James Castle and carried him back to the infirmary" (174). Furthermore, James Castle died wearing a turtleneck sweater that Holden had loaned him (170), linking the two symbolically through the use of an object signifier. Finally, it is implied that Holden may be following James Castle in unintentional ways, for Salinger is careful to have Holden reveal to the reader that "All I knew about [James Castle] was that his name was always right ahead of me at roll call. Cabel, R., Cable, W., Castle, Caulfield—I can still remember it" (171). James Castle died because he believed that it was noble never to take back one's word and thus to advance the cause of truth by speaking it and standing behind it. Ironically, Antolini's quotation from Wilhelm Stekel that "The mark of the immature man is that he wants to die nobly for a cause" echoes across Castle's death, for Castle died nobly for a cause, and Holden, by implication, can either be the next in line to die for a noble cause or be the mature man who wants "to live humbly" for a cause. If Holden's primary aversion is to avoid phonies and phony situations, James Castle's death is the lesson that teaches the price of opposing phoniness with the truth.

Holden's tenure at Pency Prep provides readers of *Catcher in the Rye* with insights into Holden's most pointed lessons concerning the peer influence typical of the sibling society. Granted, there are some other students with whom Holden spends some brief yet pleasant time; he describes, for example, tossing a football around one October evening with Robert Tichener and Paul Campbell and recalling them as "nice guys, especially Tichener" (4), and he tells of going into Agerstown to "have a hamburger and maybe see a lousy movie" with Mal Brossard, who Holden clearly identifies as "this friend of mine" (36). But that's it. Robert Ackley, who goes into Agerstown with Holden and Mal Brossard, is an example of a negative older (by two years) role model; Holden describes him as being hulking and having awful hygiene, as "one of these very, very tall, round-shouldered guys—he was about six four—with lousy teeth" and "a lot of pimples" (19). Moreover, and beyond the physical descriptions, Ackley is "a very peculiar guy" who "hardly ever went *any*where," perhaps because he was a nasty guy with a terrible personality (19); a senior and a loner, Ackley is hardly a role model for Holden. In direct contrast to Ackley is Ward Stradlater, Holden's roommate at Pency, who, though he appears as "mostly a Year Book kind of handsome guy" is really "more of a secret slob" (27). Stradlater, a kind of ward of the prep school system, is a user: he uses Holden's coat (25), his Vitalis (31), his talent by asking Holden to write an essay for him (28), and, if the implications are clear, Stradlater uses—or tries to use—Jane Gallagher for his own sexual gratification (43). The "secret slob" (27) whose sexual activities are "a professional secret" (43) is both a poor role model from the peer group of the prep school sibling society and an antithetical opposite of Holden's older brother D. B., who wrote a "terrific book of short stories, *The Secret Goldfish*" (1). Further, Stradlater wears Holden's jacket—as much an object signifier as the turtleneck sweater James Castle borrowed from Holden—during his escapade in Ed Banky's car with Jane Gallagher, making him a surrogate for Holden. Ironically, Holden's physical contact with Jane is limited to holding hands (79) and kissing her "all over—*any*where—her eyes, her *nose*, her forehead, her eyebrows and all, her *ears*—her whole face except her mouth" (79) as she cries after an encounter with Mr. Cudahy, her stepfather, and his innocent and non-exploitative actions are in direct contrast to those of Stradlater or, as is implied, even Mr. Cudahy. In essence, Holden would rather be a "bore" in this sense, one who with a "swell girl" like Jane will not "hurt anybody" (124).

In contrast to, or perhaps as an extension of, the prep school sibling society, Salinger has Holden encounter several other older males or contrasting peers, again as negative role models. One peer is "George something," who attends Andover, another prep school. When he meets with Holden and Sally at the play, he "didn't *hes*itate to horn in on my date, the bastard," says Holden, critical of how both George and Sally identify "more places and more names" (128) they have in common, which to Holden suggests identification through cliques. But what Holden finds most bothersome, the worst part, is that "the jerk had one of those very phony, Ivy League voices, one of those very tired, snobby voices. He sounded just like a girl" (128). And because in his adolescence Holden is concerned with his own sexuality, he perceives of George as effeminate. By contrast, Holden has been introduced earlier by Lillian Simmons, D. B.'s ex-girlfriend, to the Navy guy named "Commander Blop or something," whose macho image is emphasized by Holden's comment that Blop was "one of those guys that think they're being a pansy if they don't break around forty of your fingers when they shake hands with you" (86). Other older male role models, especially as they pertain to negative male role models concerning sexual knowledge, include Eddie Birdsell, from Princeton, who gives out ex-burlesque stripper Faith Cavendish's phone number to young inexperienced boys like Holden (63) and the "Joe Yale-looking Guy" at Ernie's who is giving his "terrific-looking girl" a feel under the table while talking about a guy who tried to commit suicide (85–6), a scene which evokes both Stradlater's forcing himself on Jane Gallagher and James Castle's suicide.

On the whole, Holden is outrightly critical of the student peers he encounters at Pency Prep. In fact, Salinger has Holden identify the image of Pency Prep in the novel's second paragraph, showing how its media image contrasts the physical actuality of the school: "Pency Prep...advertise[s] in about a thousand magazines, always showing some hot-shot guy on a horse jumping over a fence. Like as if all you ever did at Pency was play polo all the time. I never even once saw a horse anywhere *near* the place" (2). The ad connotes class, leisure, character, and status. Deconstructing the concept of character building at Pency Prep and schools like it, Holden adds that

> And underneath the guy on the horse's picture, it always says: "Since 1888 we have been molding boys into splendid, clear-thinking young men." Strictly for the birds. They don't do any damn more *molding* at Pency than they do at any other school. And I don't know anybody there that was splendid and clear-thinking and all. Maybe two guys. If that many. And they probably *came* to Pency that way. (2)

What is suggested here is that it is during a child's formative years at home that character, morals, and ethics are developed and that in the sibling society of the prep school environment, each adolescent manifests the character traits he has, each in his own way. And Holden is critical of these traits when he encounters them. Having had his coat and gloves stolen from his room, Holden decrees that Pency was full of crooks (4), an ironic comment considering that most of the students were from the East Coast upper class, a point not overlooked by Holden who adds that "Quite a few guys came from these very wealthy families, but it was full of crooks anyway. The more expensive a school is, the more crooks it has" (4). Moreover, he tells Phoebe that Pency was "one of the worst schools I ever went to. It was full of . . . mean guys. You never saw so many mean guys in your life" (167). One such mean guy is Earnest Morrow, whom Holden recalls as "doubtless the biggest bastard that ever went to Pency, in the whole crumby history of the school. He was always going down the corridor, after he'd had a shower, snapping his soggy old towel at people's asses" (54). Worse even than mean individuals, though, are the cliques that exclude, ostracize, or gang up on the weak individuals. Holden was aware that it was "this very conceited boy, Phil Stabile" and "about six other dirty bastards" (170) who drove James Castle to his death; what's worse is that the mean individuals group together into cliques, the antithesis of individuals with integrity, boys like James Castle and, by association, Holden. After ice skating, Holden tries to explain this aspect of life at "a boy's school" (131) to Sally Hayes:

> ...and everybody sticks together in these dirty little goddam cliques. The guys that are on the basketball team stick together, the Catholics stick together, the goddam intellectuals stick together, the guys that play bridge stick together. Even the guys that belong to the goddam Book-of-the-*Month* Club stick together. (131)

Holden tries to suggests that this grouping activity is an affront to the individual who sees through it, telling Sally that "If you try to have a little intelligent—" (131), but she—having made it clear in her conversation with George during the play that she believes that cliques are part of one's social identity—cuts Holden off before he can complete his statement. Holden indicates that the only option is to completely withdraw from such a sibling society, to go to Massachusetts and Vermont, and "live somewhere with a brook and all" (132), a vision of a place completely unlike the world of prep schools for boys in which Holden lives and from which he manages to keep getting expelled.

Christopher Brookeman's 1991 essay "Pency Preppy: Cultural Codes in *The Catcher in the Rye*" gives every indication that Pency Prep is a form of what Robert Bly would qualify as a sibling society. In considering Pency Prep as representative of single-sex boarding schools, Brookeman sees it as a place where "young future professionals of the middle and upper classes experienced an extended period of training and socialization" (59). Because students usually board, the prep school functions as "an idealized family standing in loco parentis" (61), suggesting that all students are siblings within the prep school culture of the peer group. In considering how *Catcher in the Rye* offers commentary on the changing American social character in the 1950, Brookeman points to sociologists' interest in which agencies were most influential in the socialization process, settling on the family and the peer group (63), with Salinger presenting Holden "socializing with a member or members of his peer group" (63). Most notable is Brookeman's observation regarding the result of Holden's generation being peer influenced to a greater extent than by the family influence of previous generations:

> What Salinger shows is a world in which the loafing habits of teenagers, the peer group and its culture, have become a way of life; and although Salinger does not directly moralize about his hero's condition, there is something tragic about the sadly contracted state of Holden's world from which other generations have withdrawn, leaving his own generation in its one-dimensional fate. (64)

The other generations, represented by Holden's parents and teachers, are replaced by his own generation, represented by the peer groups of the prep schools Holden attends. Further, because the peers mentor themselves, they function as a kind of sibling society, a society so pervasive that, as Brookeman notes:

> A particular aspect of Salinger's treatment of the peer group and its activities is the way Holden's brothers, D. B. and Allie, and his younger sister Phoebe are more like members of his peer group than of his family.... This closeness to his brothers and sister is in stark contrast to the relation with his parents, who are absent, shadowy figures. (71)

What Holden seeks, therefore, is an older sibling to mentor him, initiate him into adulthood, and this age dichotomy dominates *The Catcher in the Rye*.

If one reads Holden as H(old)en, it is evident that Holden seeks someone who is older as a mentor to guide him. He refers to many characters, both potential mentors and siblings, as "old," using the term as one of respect, familiarity, or intimacy. He uses the term appropriately to describe older males, as in "old Spencer, my history teacher" (*Catcher in the Rye* 3), "old Thurmer" (17), the Pency Headmaster, and "old Ossenburger"

(16) after whom Holden's dorm at Pency was named. Interestingly, he uses the adjective to describe many of the girls his own age, as in "Old Selma Thurmer—she was the headmaster's daughter" (3), "old Sally Hayes" (105), and "old Jane" Gallagher (77). Many of his peers at Pency are labeled similarly: "old Ackley" (19), "old Stradlater" (25), and even "old Marsalla" (17) the Pency student who farted during Ossenburger's talk in chapel; further, Holden remembers "old James Castle" (170) from Elkton Hills, as well as "old [Carl] Luce" (143) and the ironically labeled "old Childs" (99) the Quaker, both from Whooton School. Holden doesn't limit himself to this prep school peers, however, for he refers to "old Maurice," the pimp, and "old Sunny," the prostitute (101), and even his own younger siblings, "old Phoebe" (67) and "old Allie" (39).

In contrast to Holden's use of the word "old" as a term of specific familiarity, he is aware of his own youth. Holden states that he is prone to "act quite young for my age sometimes," and that, in fact, "sometimes I act like I'm about thirteen" (9), and even more so, Holden is aware that "I still act sometimes like I was only about twelve. Everybody says that, especially my father" (9). These ages are important, in that Holden was thirteen when Allie, who was eleven, died; it seems that, because "Life stopped for Holden on July 18, 1946, the day his brother died of leukemia," as Edwin Haviland Miller notes, Holden "is emotionally still the same age [thirteen]" (132). In this way, Holden has a kind of arrested emotional development, remaining the emotional age he was when his brother died, as if remaining at this (emotional) age could keep Allie closer to him. In addition, Phoebe, ten at the time of the events narrated in *Catcher in the Rye*, is one year younger than Allie was when he died. Holden is caught in this age contradiction with various peers during the course of the novel. At Pency Prep, for example, Ackley, who was always telling Holden that he was a kid, was angered himself when Holden called him "Ackley kid" (*Catcher in the Rye* 21). Holden, who, when in New York, stands to order drinks and turns his few gray hairs toward the waiters, does so because he is all too aware that he is still a minor (70). When Holden asks Sally Hayes to run away with him "up to Massachusetts and Vermont," she is quick to remind him that they are "both practically *children*" (132). Meeting Carl Luce, his logical mentor, Holden is asked by Luce, when they first meet, when he is going to grow up (144), followed by Luce's comment that Holden's mind is immature (147). Then Antolini passes on to Holden the Wilhelm Stekel quotation concerning maturity and immaturity (188), implying that Holden's immaturity is the current problem. Holden is left, alone at Grand Central Station, reading a magazine article about hormones, indicating Holden's lingering interest in finding some scientific explanation for his immaturity:

> It [the magazine] described how you should look, your face and eyes and all, if your hormones were in good shape, and I didn't look that way at all. I looked exactly like the guy in the article with lousy hormones. (195)

Poor Holden: he no more matches the visual image of the mature adolescent shown in the magazine than he matches Stekel's definition of the mature man! No wonder, then, that Holden's "sense of alienation is almost complete—from parents, from friends, from society in general as represented by the prep school from which he has be expelled" (Jones 24). What completes his alienation, his own profound recognition that he is mentorless himself, occurs when Phoebe wishes to run away with him. He sees her, as if in a mirror, arriving with Holden's "crazy hunting hat on" (205) and dragging Holden's "old suitcase, the one I used when I was at Whooton" (206). In that moment, he seems to realize that he has become an older sibling mentor to his own little sister, Phoebe, much in the same way that his older brother, D. B., is a mentor to him.

A short time later, Holden, sitting on a bench by the carrousel like the other kids' parents, projects an image of himself as a surrogate parent. Having assumed the role of mentor, having moved further through the door to adulthood, Holden is able to grasp, in a near-epiphany, by watching Phoebe on the carrousel, what he himself has been going through:

> All the kids kept trying to grab for the gold ring, and so was old Phoebe, and I was sort of afraid she'd fall off the goddam horse, but I didn't say anything or do

anything. The thing with kids is, if they want to grab for the gold ring, you have to
let them do it, and not say anything. If they fall off, they fall off.... (211)

From his new perspective as older mentor, Holden can see that adolescence
is a time for reaching for gold rings and that falling off while doing so is
often a part of the process.

Throughout the novel, Holden's alienation and awareness of his own
lack of maturity have had him seeking an *older* person to mentor him. As
Robert Bly suggests, however, the sibling society "offers very little
generosity or support to young men" (*Sibling Society* 129). Holden, therefore,
struggles in the book because he is unable to "invest his trust in anyone
who is not an image of innocence," that is, those he deems phony; as a
result, he "has no guides or teachers whom he can accept" (Bloom 6).
Robert Bly's concern is that in the sibling society, both with its blurred
distinction between adolescents and adults and with its absence of visible
adult mentors, that too many of the young—and this would include Holden
Caulfield—are "forced to become adults too soon, and never make it"
(*Sibling Society* 132). Hope, concludes Bly, lies in "tak[ing] an interest in
younger ones by helping them find a mentor" so that "their own feeling of
being adult will be augmented" (237). As such, Holden Caulfield, a "typical"
adolescent of the 1950s, becomes a prototype of the troubled, aimless
young men Bly sees evident in the *fin de siècle*'s sibling society. Perhaps, then,
what troubled critics of *Catcher in the Rye* most was not so much what they
saw evident in Holden but what they suspected in the coming tide of social
disruption which he represented. Holden's "breakdown" at the end of the
novel is therefore endemic of the societal breakdown in adolescent
transition currently occurring, based, in part, upon the loss of effective male
mentors for young men, upon the "death" of the mentor.

For Holden, his hope may be in reconnecting with his older sibling, D.
B., who, by the final chapter, lives close enough to drive over to visit
Holden, suggesting that Holden has been intentionally relocated (by his
parents?) to be closer to his brother. On the one hand, Holden's father has
had his way: Holden is working with "this one psychoanalyst guy they have
here," presumably getting the therapy to deal with Allie's death, which has

affected him and which he has not effectively dealt with. On the other hand, D. B. may be Holden's necessary mentor; unlike everyone else who "keeps asking me if I'm going to apply myself when I go back to school next September," D. B., who "isn't as bad as the rest of them," instead asks Holden "what I thought about all this stuff I just finished telling you about" (*Catcher in the Rye* 213). Holden's response is interesting: "I didn't know what the hell to say" (213), for Holden up until now hasn't had anyone who would just listen to him, ask his opinion, help him find the patterns of his own mind, in short, be an adult mentor who helps augment Holden's feelings of being an adult.

WORKS CITED

Baumbach, Jonathan. "The Saint as a Young Man: A Reappraisal of *The Catcher in the Rye*." *Modern Language Quarterly* 25:4 (December 1964): 461–72. Rpt. in *Critical Essays on Salinger's* The Catcher in the Rye. Ed. Joel Salzberg. Boston: G. K. Hall, 1990. 55–63.

Bloom, Harold. Introduction. *J. D. Salinger's* The Catcher in the Rye*: Bloom's Notes*. Broomall, PA: Chelsea House, 1996. 5–6.

Bly, Robert. *Iron John*. Reading, MA: Addison-Wesley, 1990.

———. *The Sibling Society*. Reading, MA: Addison-Wesley, 1996.

Brookeman, Christopher. "Pency Preppy: Cultural Codes in *The Catcher in the Rye*." *New Essays on* The Catcher in the Rye. Ed. Jack Salzman. Cambridge: Cambridge University Press, 1991. 57–76.

Bryson, Bill. *Made in America: An Informal History of the English Language in the United States*. New York: William Morrow, 1994.

Hughes, Riley. "New Novels." *Catholic World* 1040 (November 1951): 154. Rpt. in *Holden Caulfield*. Ed. Harold Bloom. New York: Chelsea House Publishers, 1990. 8.

Jones, Ernest. "Case History of All of Us." *Nation* 173:9 (1 September 1951): 176. Rpt. in *Critical Essays on Salinger's* The Catcher in the Rye. Ed. Joel Salzberg. Boston: G. K. Hall, 1990. 55–63.

Longstreth, T. Morris. "New Novels in the News." *Christian Science Monitor* (19 July 1951): 11. Rpt. in *Holden Caulfield.* Ed. Harold Bloom. New York: Chelsea House Publishers, 1990. 5–6.

Miller, Edwin Haviland. "In Memoriam: Allie Caulfield." *Mosaic* 15:1 (Winter 1982): 129–40. Rpt. in *Holden Caulfield.* Ed. Harold Bloom. New York: Chelsea House, 1990. 132–43.

Rice, Philip F. *The Adolescent: Development, Relationships, and Culture.* 6th Ed. Boston, Allyn and Bacon, 1990.

Rosen, Gerald. "A Retrospective Look at *The Catcher in the Rye.*" *American Quarterly* 5 (Winter 1977): 547–62. Rpt. in *Critical Essays on Salinger's* The Catcher in the Rye. Ed. Joel Salzberg. Boston: G. K. Hall, 1990. 158–71.

Rowe, Joyce. "Holden Caulfield and American Protest." *New Essays on* The Catcher in the Rye. Ed. Jack Salzman. Cambridge: Cambridge University Press, 1991. 77–95.

Salinger, J. D. *Franny and Zooey.* Boston: Little, Brown and Co., 1961.

———. *The Catcher in the Rye.* Boston: Little, Brown and Company, 1991.

3.

Catcher in the Corn:
J. D. Salinger and *Shoeless Joe*

DENNIS CUTCHINS

One of the most interesting treatments of J. D. Salinger's work in recent years has been W. P. Kinsella's novel *Shoeless Joe*. Kinsella's first novel must be understood, at least in part, as a complex and sustained response to *Catcher in the Rye*. The Canadian author establishes a strong affinity between Holden Caulfield, Shoeless Joe Jackson, and his own semiautobiographical Ray Kinsella. Kinsella, the writer, even uses J. D. Salinger as a character in his novel, blurring the line between reality and fiction as well as the line between the legal and the illegal. Salinger's appearance in the novel should be understood, however, as more than gratuitous name dropping, or what Kinsella referred to in an interview as "audacious" risk taking (Dahlin 7). Each of his major characters, including "Jerry Salinger," faces a crisis of faith, a set of dilemmas that may be generally understood as the conflict between idealism and reality, and in this theme Kinsella was apparently responding to *Catcher*. Arthur Heiserman and James E. Miller, Jr. in "J. D. Salinger: Some Crazy Cliff," one of the first scholarly treatments of *Catcher*, suggest that readers must understand the novel in terms of this conflict between idealism and reality, and their essay sets a tone which polarized much later criticism.[1] Readers of the novel should focus not on Holden, they argue, but rather on the world in which Holden lives, concluding that the "book's last ironic incongruity" is that "It is not Holden who should be examined for a sickness of the mind, but the world in which he has sojourned and found himself an alien" (38). Gerald Rosen reiterates this idea and goes so far as to call *Catcher in the Rye* a "novel of the death of belief in America" (96). Kinsella seems to accept this general interpretation of *Catcher*, and he proceeds to follow Heiserman, Miller, and Rosen in examining the modern world for a "sickness of the mind," and "the death of belief." *Shoeless Joe* goes beyond *Catcher*, however, in that it offers a possible cure for this modern illness.

Although *Shoeless Joe* is a successful novel and work of art in its own right, it makes the most sense when read in the context of *Catcher in the Rye*. Kinsella's book is, at least in part, an attempt to interpret, respond to, and even redeem Salinger's most famous work by affirming and rewarding the kind of idealism exemplified by Holden. Beliefs and desires, for both Holden and Ray, form an antithetical and paradoxical relationship with harsh reality. The paradox is created in large measure as the characters recognize their own complicity in the corrupt world. Using this idea of complicity as a partial basis for his argument, John Seelye suggests that *Catcher* "provided an American counterpart to European existential texts like Sartre's *Nausea* and Camus's *The Stranger*" (24). Jack Salzman, however, believes that there is a distinct difference between *Catcher* and other more strictly existentialist texts: "Salinger's strength as a writer is not his *appreciation* of life's absurdities and ultimate paradox; rather, it is his *struggle against such appreciation*" (17, emphasis added). Both Holden and Ray reject absurdity and seek, somewhat desperately, for meaning in the chaotic, dangerous, and callous worlds in which they live. They want to be peaceful, but they constantly encounter violence. They need spirituality, but they are disenchanted by the hollowness of religion. They seek family support, but their families are largely dysfunctional. And both characters face the age-old conflict between materialism and art.

Holden's search for a meaningful world is, arguably, fruitless. In the words of Joyce Rowe, "Because Holden is never allowed to imagine or experience himself in any *significant* struggle with others... neither he (nor his creator) can conceive of society as a source of growth, or self-knowledge" (90, emphasis added). Ray, on the other hand, lives in a universe that is deeply meaningful, one in which social interaction can definitely lead to growth and self-knowledge, and this may be the most important difference between the two works. Ray's outwardly strange, and even bizarre behavior eventually leads to reconciliation with both his estranged brother and his dead father. He helps ex-ballplayer Archie Graham discover meaning and reason in his life of quiet service. He helps a genuine "phoney" like Eddie Scissons turn his lies into truths. With Ray's assistance, even Shoeless Joe Jackson can be redeemed from his one great mistake. Ray's universe, the world created by Kinsella in part as a response to *Catcher in the Rye*, is not governed by random chance, insoluble paradox, or simple absurdity but by events whose interconnections are so complex as to appear random, paradoxical, or absurd.

Shoeless Joe is something of a nostalgic novel, dealing with the wishes and regrets of half a dozen or so characters and allowing them each a second chance at the road not taken. The narrator of the novel, Ray Kinsella, is an ex-insurance salesman and a serious baseball fan who moves with his wife Annie and daughter Karin to Iowa, buys a small farm, and begins growing corn.[2] In a plot made familiar by the successful film *Field of Dreams* (1989), Ray is told by a mystical voice to plow under part of his cornfield and build a baseball diamond so that his father's childhood hero, Shoeless Joe Jackson, can return from the dead and play baseball again with his teammates from the 1919 Chicago White Sox. Ray builds the field, and Jackson does come. But the erstwhile farmer is soon ordered by the voice to "Ease his pain." He instinctively knows that he is being asked to take reclusive writer J. D. Salinger to a baseball game. Ray discovers an interview Salinger had supposedly given in which he regrets not having the chance to play baseball for the New York Giants on the Polo Grounds. Ray once again obeys the voice. He finds the elderly Salinger at first a reluctant victim of his enthusiasm, then later an eager participant in his odd quest. At the behest of a third voice, the two leave for Chisholm, Minnesota, home of the deceased Doctor Archie Graham. Ray and "Jerry" interview the inhabitants of the small town and learn all they can about the doctor who, in his younger years, played a single inning of professional baseball. They eventually invite the resurrected Graham back to Iowa to play on Ray's field.

In the course of this unlikely picaresque novel, Ray, like Holden, faces some of the unpleasant realities of contemporary America. He is menaced by street thugs on Chicago's South Side, held at gunpoint in Cleveland, and knocked unconscious in Boston. Back at home, Ray's real estate mogul/brother-in-law, Mark, is busy buying all the farms in Johnson County, Iowa, and sending the simple rural folk off to live in the city. Mark and his partner, Bluestein,[3] are intent on creating a gigantic "computer farm" that will be run by a single computer operator and an army of mechanized planters and harvesters. Ray's 160 acres are the only thing standing in the way of this antipastoral nightmare, and Mark holds the mortgage. To make matters even more complex, on his return home, with Salinger still in tow, Ray discovers that his estranged twin brother, Richard, a carnival hawker and owner of a dilapidated freak show, has come to Iowa to find him. In the novel's conclusion, Ray defeats Mark, keeps the farm, and reconciles relations with both his brother and his dead father, a minor league catcher and another of the ghostly baseball players. Salinger's character is allowed to visit the afterlife with the deceased players, happy, we are led to believe, in a place where publishers, reporters, and fans can never follow.

The novel received mixed reviews. William Plummer's estimation was typical:

> It's easy enough to find fault with this wonderfully hokey first novel by a Canadian short-story writer of some repute. The language sometimes melts in the hand rather than the heart, the subplots are a hasty pudding, the Salinger of the book is not smart or quirky enough to have written about Holden Caulfield or Seymour Glass. But such complaints seem mean-spirited, tin-eared, in the face of the novel's lovely minor music. (64)

Other reviewers were not as generous in their estimation. Ian Pearson calls the novel "too contrived to be seductive..., too sluggish to work as a madcap picaresque" (61). Most readers, however, found something worthwhile in the book, and a few found more than that.[4]

Shoeless Joe and *Catcher in the Rye* have some obvious connections. Both novels are written as first-person narratives, with voices that are warm, personal, and perhaps each book's most compelling feature. Two of the main characters in *Shoeless Joe*, Richard and Ray Kinsella, are both characters from Salinger's canon. Richard Kinsella is the boy who kept digressing during Holden's Oral Expression class in *Catcher*, and Ray Kinsella, modeled after Salinger himself, is the lead character in "A Young Girl in 1941 with No Waist at All." The most compelling shared feature of the two novels, however, is the theme of innocent idealism in conflict with harsh reality. Both novels place peaceful and more or less innocent characters in the midst of societal corruption and decay. On his way to Comiskey Field in Chicago, for instance, Ray meets two teenaged girls who warn him that he is about to be robbed. "Hey, man," one calls, "you better watch out. There's some boys in the doorway of that block up there; they's figuring to rob you" (44). The other girl adds, "We don't want to see you get in any trouble. If you got any money on you, you better cross the street" (45). Ray considers taking their advice but suddenly worries that they may be setting him up. "What if the boys are on the other side of the road," he wonders, "and don't want to waste their time mugging a broke white man?" (45). Ray decides not to cross the road, and discovers, as he continues down the block, that the girls probably had been in collusion with the potential muggers. For Ray, the threat of being mugged in Chicago, along with a later encounter with a would-be armed robber in Cleveland, mirror Holden's experience with Maurice and Sunny, another thug-teenage girl partnership. Both Holden and Ray find themselves too innocent and naive to understand the dangerous worlds they face. Ray certainly experiences the "sickness" of American society and is all the more ready, when the time comes, to return to the rural Iowa countryside. For Holden, however, this violent world is home. There is no pastoral Iowa to which he may retreat. The closest he can come is Central Park, and the park, with its homeless ducks and graffiti-covered walls, is little comfort.

Both novels may be considered contemporary picaresques with the two protagonists on quests for a kind of fulfilment or meaning lacking in their mundane worlds. Heiserman and Miller may have been the first to dub *Catcher* a quest novel. They note, "We use the medieval term because it signifies a seeking after what is tremendous" (32). The tremendous or extraordinary thing Holden seeks is, at least in part, the chance to serve as a savior for misguided children. In the chaotic world he inhabits, his desire to save others reflects a powerful and moving kind of idealism. Holden's basic optimism may be roughly summed up in the title passage from the novel. When Phoebe asks her brother what he would like to be, Holden imagines himself standing in a field of rye, saving children from falling over a cliff (173). Holden's dream of saving children, however, is simply not possible in the world Salinger creates. The teenager is forced, instead, to become, in the words of Jonathan Baumbach, "an impotent savior" (62). Baumbach contends that "since it is spiritually as well as physically impossible to prevent the Fall, Salinger's idealistic heroes are doomed" to failure (56).

Where Holden fails, Ray succeeds. The field he creates literally saves the *souls* of several characters in the novel as they are able to come back to life and fulfil their dreams. He becomes a savior or "catcher" not in a field of rye but on a baseball field built in the middle of an Iowa cornfield. The novel's title character, Joe Jackson, loved to play baseball and was crushed by the ruling of Commissioner Kenesaw Mountain Landis that permanently suspended him from the game. The fictional Jackson compares the lifetime suspension to "having a part of me amputated, slick and smooth and painless" (14). A moment later he adds, "I loved the game. ...I'd have played for food money. I'd have played free and worked for food. It was the game" (15). Ray's baseball field gives Joe a second chance to play ball and to be absolved of the mistakes he made the first time around. This theme of redemption certainly does not end with Joe. Ray and Salinger discover that Archie "Moonlight" Graham died years earlier, without ever returning to baseball. He had, instead, moved to his hometown of Chisholm, Minnesota, and become a poorly paid high school doctor. During their visit to Chisholm, Salinger concludes that he and Ray had been sent to Minnesota to discover "if one inning can change the world" (152). They decide to leave with that mystery still unsolved, but on the way out of town they stop to pick up a young hitchhiker. The teenaged boy turns out to be Graham, who has come back to life to fulfil his dream of playing ball with his heroes.

Graham is able to play on Ray's field, but his subplot also suggests another kind of fulfilment. Though he seems pleased with the chance to join the team, Graham soon discovers that his life as a doctor and mentor to young people was, ultimately, more satisfying than playing professional baseball. In what is probably the novel's most touching moment, Ray's daughter, Karin, falls off of the bleachers while watching a game and begins to choke on a piece of hot dog. While the other characters stand around helplessly, the young Moonlight Graham strides confidently off of the baseball field, in the process transforming into the elderly "Doc" Graham. He quickly helps the girl, saving her life and simultaneously sacrificing his chances to play ball on the magical field. He makes, in other words, virtually the same decision he had made earlier in his life: to become a doctor rather than a ballplayer. Once again, Kinsella's novel replaces apparent absurdity with reassuring meaning. Graham's decision to help Karin affirms his career choice, giving his life a sense of intentionality and usefulness which is the very essence of meaning.

Graham's character is based partly on the real Moonlight Graham, and, I would argue, partly on a similar character in *Catcher*. At the beginning of Salinger's novel, Holden visits his history teacher, Mr. Spencer, to say goodbye. Spencer, like Graham, has spent most of his adult life working at a school, and even Holden can tell that the old teacher genuinely cares about the boys. Spencer is, after all, the only teacher he visits before leaving Pencey. But the old man seems powerless to help the boy. Holden is struck throughout the interview by Spencer's age and relative poverty: "You wondered what the heck he was still living for" (6). It never crosses the young man's mind that the Spencers are apparently happily married and that they seem more or less satisfied with their lot in life. Nor does Holden really appreciate Spencer's attempts to help him. The old teacher laments, "I'm trying to help you. I'm trying to *help* you, if I can" (14). "He really was, too. You could see that," Holden admits, "But it was just that we were too much on opposite sides of the pole, that's all" (14–15). Spencer's final "Good luck" is particularly annoying to Holden. "I'd never yell 'Good luck!' at anybody," he notes. "It sounds terrible, when you think about it" (16). Holden perceives Spencer's work at the school as well meaning but ultimately futile and worthless, another set of absurd acts in the trivial world he inhabits. Ray, on the other hand, comes to see Graham's life of service to young people as both good and useful. Graham had filled his life in Chisholm with quiet labor for his neighbors and his students. "There were times when children could not afford eyeglasses or milk, or clothing because of the economic upheavals, strikes and depressions," Ray reads in Graham's obituary. "Yet no child was ever denied these essentials, because in the background, there was a benevolent, understanding Doctor Graham" (123). Graham's life, a mirror image of Spencer's, is judged, finally, to be worthwhile.

Certainly the word most often associated with *Catcher in the Rye* is "phoney." Holden first applies the term to Headmaster Haas and to the returning alumnus Ossenburger as a result of the discrepancy he perceives between their public face and their private action. Holden is bothered by the fact that Haas pretends to like wealthy or handsome parents but acts very differently toward middle-class or poorly dressed parents:

> On Sundays, for instance, old Haas went around shaking hands with everybody's parents when they drove up to school. He'd be charming as hell and all. Except if some boy had little old funny-looking parents.... I mean if a boy's mother was sort of fat or corny-looking or something, and if somebody's father was one of those guys that wear those suits with very big shoulders and corny black and white shoes, then old Haas would just shake hands with them and give them a phony smile and then he'd go talk, for maybe a half an *hour*, with somebody else's parents. (14)

Like Haas, Ossenburger also misrepresents himself. At chapel he gives a speech, starting "with about fifty corny jokes, just to show us what a regular guy he was" (16). The undertaker then proceeds to describe his own humility and lack of pride. Yet all of this is belied in Holden's mind by the fact that Ossenburger "made a pot of dough in the undertaking business," and drives a "big goddam Cadillac" (16).

In *Shoeless Joe*, Kinsella does not use the term "phony," but he does include one character who, like Haas and Ossenburger, utterly misrepresents himself. Eddie Scissons, the retired farmer who sells his land and equipment to Ray and Annie, first impresses Ray with his claims to be "the oldest living Chicago Cub" (42). Ray soon discovers, though, that none of Eddie's stories are true and that he never played major league baseball. For years he has lied to his friends and neighbors about a nonexistent career. Ray, nevertheless, keeps Eddie's secret. "I understand Eddie Scissons," he explains. "I know that some of us, and for some reason I am one of them, get to reach out and touch our heart's desire," while others "are rewarded with snarls, frustration, and disillusionment" (218). When the truth about Eddie is later revealed by Mark, the old man is crushed. Once again, however, Ray's field provides an answer. As Ray and the others, including Eddie, watch one of the ghostly games, they realize that "Kid Scissons" has been called in as a relief pitcher. The fans watch as Eddie's lies are made true. His dream of playing for the Cubs is enacted before their eyes. Kid Scissons plays poorly, though, and his mistakes cost the Cubs the game. The old man takes the double humiliation philosophically. Later he reveals to Ray, "I heard somebody say once, 'Success is getting what you want, but happiness is wanting what you get'" (230). He adds, "You saw what happened to me. I got what I wanted, but it wasn't what I needed to make me happy" (230). In Kinsella's world, even phonies get the chance to be redeemed.

Perhaps the worst kind of phonies, for both Holden and Ray, are religious ones. At the same time, however, both protagonists feel a strong need for a sense of spirituality. Jonathan Baumbach dubs *Catcher* "a religious or, to be more exact, spiritual novel" (59). Holden's feelings about *organized* religion, though, are most succinctly expressed in his discussion of Jesus and the Disciples:

> I like Jesus and all, but I don't care too much for most of the other stuff in the
> Bible. Take the Disciples, for instance. They annoy the hell out of me, if you want

to know the truth…. While He was alive, they were about as much use to him as a
hole in the head. All they did was keep letting Him down. (99)

The Disciples' main problem, at least as Holden sees it, is their intolerance
and inability to forgive: "Jesus never sent old Judas to Hell," he argues. "I
think any one of the Dis*ci*ples would've sent him to Hell and all—and fast,
too—but I'll bet anything Jesus didn't do it" (100). Modern Christians also
come under fire for their intolerance, or potential intolerance, as well as
their hypocrisy. Holden worries, for instance, that the nuns he meets at
Grand Central Station will "all of a sudden try to find out if I was a
Catholic" (112). Other clergy, too, fall under his condemnation. "If you
want to know the truth," he allows, "I can't even stand ministers. The ones
they've had at every school I've gone to, they have these Holy Joe voices
when they start giving their sermons. God, I hate that. I don't see why the
hell they can't talk in their natural voice" (100).

Ray has similar feelings about clergy and religious folk. He makes a
point of mentioning Thaddeus Cridge, the Episcopal bishop of Iowa,
whose apartment after his death contained "2000 pounds of pornographic
magazines and books, as well as a number of albums full of compromising
photographs of Cridge and neighborhood children" (115). Ray is also quite
critical of Annie's family's outward appearance of religiousness and inner
reality of intolerance and prejudice:

> The kind of people I absolutely cannot tolerate are those, like Annie's mother,
> who never let you forget they are religious. It seems to me that a truly religious
> person would let his life be example enough, would not let his religion interfere
> with being a human being, and would not be so insecure as to have to fawn
> publicly before his gods. (175)

Kinsella can rarely pass up a chance to make fun of those who profess to
be religious. When Ray first comes to Iowa, the woman who is to become
his mother-in-law at first rejects him as a renter because he was not a
practicing Christian. He ends up getting the room, however, because "it
was early October, her Christian roomer had been cut by the football team

and had left for Georgia, after kicking a hole in his door and writing misspelled four-letter words on the wall with a crayon" (176). Like Holden, however, Ray feels a need for the spiritual. His answer to that need, in fact, his answer to most of the problems faced in the novel, is baseball. He advocates the building of roadside shrines to baseball greats, suggests that "a ballpark at night is more like a church than a church," and, noting the fans at a game, points out, "We're not just ordinary people, we're a congregation. Baseball is a ceremony, a ritual" (34, 160, 84). Holden may be denied spirituality, but Ray finds his spiritual needs satisfied by a secular game.

Shoeless Joe resembles *Catcher* on structural and thematic levels, but Kinsella's use of J. D. Salinger as a character expands and complicates *Shoeless Joe*'s response to *Catcher in the Rye*. Kinsella uses the characters of Salinger and Joe Jackson, in particular, as metaphors to explore the very nature of public life in America and the relationship between artistry and integrity. He asks what it means to be a "hero" in this country and questions the responsibilities of public life. Certainly these questions resonate, both in context of Salinger's life and in terms of his most famous work.

Kinsella's use of Salinger as a fictional character raised more than a few eyebrows. One reviewer suggested that for Kinsella to put his "own words into a living person's mouth is merely presumptuous, not clever" (Pearson 59). Kinsella himself has never fully explained his incorporation of Salinger, telling one interviewer, "I didn't know I was going to use Salinger…. It was just something in the back of my head. I like being audacious" (Dahlin 7). He added, "I can't imagine him being terribly upset…. He's portrayed as a compassionate character, and, as a matter of fact, this is something I took great pains to do" (7).[5]

One reason for Kinsella's use of the older author may be the fairly mundane fact that Salinger had recently been in the news when Kinsella wrote his novel. In 1974, the reclusive author sued several bookstores for selling an unauthorized, anonymously published collection of his early fiction. In November of that year, Salinger gave his first interview in over twenty years. Speaking on the phone to Lacey Fosburgh, a San Francisco reporter, Salinger said, "There is a marvelous peace in not publishing. It's peaceful. Still. Publishing is a terrible invasion of my privacy" (Fosburgh 1). At the end of the interview he added, "I pay for this kind of attitude. I'm known as a strange, aloof kind of man. But all I'm doing is trying to protect myself and my work" (69). Five years later, in July of 1979 in Windsor, Vermont, Salinger gave an impromptu interview to "a college-age couple" who had stopped him in the street to ask questions. A photographer quickly took a picture of the famous author and asked the couple what Salinger had told them. They replied that he had asked them not to discuss their conversation but noted, "He told us not to take anybody's advice, including his, and that it's very important to read" (13). Kinsella would have been working on *Shoeless Joe* at the time, and the title of the *Newsweek* article may have been another inspiration as he worked on his homage to baseball. A clever editor gave the article an unintended baseball twist when he or she named it "Dodger in the Rye."[6]

In the summer of 1980 Salinger gave yet another interview, this time to Betty Eppes, a perky tennis player and features writer for the Baton Rouge *Advocate*. A longer version of the interview was published in the *Paris Review* in the summer of 1981 and would certainly have been noticed by Kinsella as he finished *Shoeless Joe*. In that interview Salinger told Eppes that he was writing, though he had no intentions to publish, and reiterated his plea to be left in peace. His wish, however, was not to be granted. On December 8, 1980, Mark David Chapman shot John Lennon in the back as the rock star entered his New York apartment. A few months later, in February 1981, Chapman gave a statement to the *New York Times* which stressed the importance of Salinger's *Catcher in the Rye*. He claimed that the novel itself was the best statement of his intentions as he shot Lennon. It was in this highly charged context that Kinsella wrote and published *Shoeless Joe*.

Salinger's appearances in the news, however, do not fully explain his existence as a character in *Shoeless Joe*. Kinsella saw a deeper relationship between the aging literary icon and Joe Jackson. There is little doubt that Salinger is a compelling individual. His life since the publication of *Catcher* has literally rewritten the book on the division between public and private life. Salinger's decision to avoid public life over the past forty years has shrouded the man in mystery and given his works an almost mythical quality. In creating the fictional Salinger, Kinsella worked to answer two of the most basic dilemmas facing public figures: how can one be a private individual in a very public field? and how can one have integrity as a writer and, at the same time, be a producer of consumer goods? Kinsella notes the relationship between baseball players and writers in a 1987 interview:

> A baseball player is only as good as his last fifty at-bats, an author is only as good as his last book. The work each does is mercilessly scrutinized by critics and the public. In both professions only the wily, the ruthlessly ambitious, and those with eyes for the absurd have long careers. (Horvath and Palmer 190)

Salinger addresses these same questions several times in *Catcher in the Rye*. Charles Kaplan noted this theme in 1956, suggesting that the novel explored what he called "the relationship between virtuosity and integrity" (43). Joyce Rowe echoes Kaplan and adds, "From beginning to end of his journey, from school to sanitarium, Holden's voice, alternating between obscenity and delicacy, conveys his rage at the inability of his contemporaries to transcend the corrosive materialism of modern American life" (78). She argues that "the bathos of American society turns out to be the real illness from which Holden suffers" (82). In *Shoeless Joe*, Kinsella agrees with and dramatizes Rowe's interpretations, but he also suggests, in the words of James E. Miller, that "Holden's sickness of soul is something deeper than economic or political ills, that his revulsion at life is not limited to social and monetary inequities, but at something in the nature of life itself" (142).

Certainly the materialism and triviality of American art are two of the most important themes of *Catcher*; Salinger returned to them several times in the course of Holden's narration. In the opening paragraph of the book, Holden sets up the dilemma between materialism and art when he mentions that his brother, D. B., has given up his literary writing career, moved to Hollywood, and become "a prostitute" by writing for the film industry (2). The primary issue for Holden in the case of his brother seems to be money and its potential effect on D. B.'s art. He makes a point of mentioning D. B.'s new Jaguar and the fact that "He's got a lot of dough, now. [though] He didn't *use* to" (1). It's important to note that Holden doesn't suggest that his brother lacks talent as a writer, acknowledging, "he wrote this terrific book of short stories," but rather laments D. B.'s willingness to write *for money*. In Holden's mind the roles of creative artist and producer of consumer goods are mutually exclusive.

Film and stage actors come to represent, in the course of the novel, the very teeth of this dilemma. "I hate actors," Holden notes. "They never act like people" (117). For Holden, the causes of bad acting (and herein lies the dilemma) are the performer's awareness of an audience and simultaneous knowledge that he or she is a famous actor. "And if any actor's really good," he explains, "you can always tell he *knows* he's good, and that spoils it" (117). Holden notes that Alfred Lunt and Lynn Fontanne, two actors he sees in a Broadway play "didn't act like people and they didn't act like actors…. They acted more like they knew they were celebrities and all. I mean they were good, but they were *too* good" (126). "If you do something too good," he added, "then after a while, if you don't watch it, you start showing off. And then you're not good anymore" (126).

Holden's critique applies to other kinds of performers as well. Perhaps he is most critical of Ernie, the Greenwich Village nightclub owner and piano player. As with the Lunts and D.B., Ernie's skill is not in question. "He's so good," Holden notes, "he's almost corny" (80). The problem is the audience's effect on Ernie: "I don't even think he *knows* any more when he's playing right or not. It isn't his fault. I partly blame all those dopes that clap their heads off—they'd foul up *any*body, if you gave them a chance" (84). Holden's solution to the problem is for the artist to completely withdraw from public performance. Though not practical, it gets to the heart of the problem facing all public figures. "If I were a piano player or an actor or something and all those dopes thought I was terrific, I'd hate it. I wouldn't even want them to *clap* for me. People always clap for the wrong things. If I were a piano player, I'd play it in the goddam closet" (84). Later, at a different performance, he adds, "If you sat around there long enough and heard all the phonies applauding and all, you got to hate everybody in the world" (142). Holden's "solution" exposes his basic inability to compromise on this question. For him, this issue is black and white, right and wrong. The problem of art and materialism is, like other problems in the novel, practically insoluble in Holden's world.

The one performer Holden praises is so obscure as to avoid any public recognition. He thus remains a "pure" artist. To kill time before his appointment with Carl Luce, Holden goes to Radio City Music Hall to see a movie. He arrives in time for the floor show but is disappointed by the Rockettes "kicking their heads off" and a roller skating performer: "I couldn't enjoy it much because I kept picturing him *practi*cing to be a guy that roller skates on the stage" (137). Finally Holden notes the kettle drummer in the orchestra. "He's the best drummer I ever saw," Holden bubbles. "He only gets a chance to bang them a couple of times during the whole piece, but he never looks bored when he isn't doing it. Then when he does bang them, he does it so nice and sweet, with this nervous expression on his face" (138). For Holden, only performers like the kettle drummer, who are able to avoid public attention, remain true artists. Through these characters, Salinger gives a fairly coherent warning, all the more powerful because of his own withdrawal from the public eye, about the danger of mixing public acclaim and private art.

Once again, Kinsella's characters echo the dilemma found in *Catcher*, but there are alternatives in *Shoeless Joe* not available in Salinger's novel. Rather than focus on actors and musical performers, Kinsella deals primarily with ball players like Joe Jackson. As with the star performers Salinger depicts, Joe is the best at what he does. With a lifetime batting average of .356 and legendary play in the field, Jackson was one of the finest ever to play the game. By 1919, however, baseball was making the transition from an amateur sport to a big business, and Kinsella notes that, even at this early date, the game had fallen victim to capitalism. "The players," he argues, "were paid peasant salaries while the owners became rich" (9). Given the popularity of baseball, and the money involved, it is little wonder that the sport attracted the attention of businessmen, gamblers, and crooks. The White Sox were heavy favorites to win the 1919 World Series when gamblers[7] convinced several of the players to "throw" the contest. Eight players on the Chicago team, including Jackson, were later accused of accepting bribe money to lose. Jackson, meanwhile, batted .375 in the series, leading all hitters and knocking a home run in the last game, the only one hit by either team. The other players involved, owner Comiskey, and even the gamblers accused of instigating the "fix," all testified that Jackson was innocent of wrongdoing, but despite strong evidence in his favor, Jackson was barred for life from playing major league baseball. He died in 1951, his name still synonymous with dishonesty. In this historical figure, Kinsella finds a strong resonance with the tainted performers Holden encounters in *Catcher*. In the words of Kinsella, "Shoeless Joe became a symbol of the tyranny of the powerful over the powerless," as well as a living, breathing example of the conflict between artistic performance and materialism (Kinsella 7). Unlike D. B., Ernie, or the Lunts, however, Joe is given a second chance, an opportunity to play on Ray's field for the pure love of the game—not for the fans, and not for the money. He enjoys a kind of redemption that is simply not possible in Holden's world.

The final major connection between these two novels is their treatment of family. Family relationships are important in *Catcher in the Rye*, particularly sibling relationships. Holden's idolization of Allie, his love for Phoebe, and his regret for the lifestyle D. B. has chosen form much of the text of the novel.[8] He desperately misses Allie, calling him the most intelligent and "nicest" member of the family (38). Holden's love for his younger brother has not weakened, despite the child's death. He exclaims to Phoebe in a moment of frustration (and insensitivity), "Just because somebody's dead, you don't just stop liking them, for God's sake— especially if they were about a thousand times nicer than the people you know that're alive and all" (171). His relationship to Phoebe is also close, and his conversation with her in D. B.'s room forms the emotional core of the novel. Though Holden has yearned for someone to talk to throughout the first two-thirds of the narrative, calling a succession of friends on the telephone, this is his first *honest* conversation. When Phoebe asks him what he truly likes, he can only think of two things—Allie, and talking with her (171). Their relationship serves as the anchor that keeps him from completely abandoning his old life. After Holden makes up his mind to run away, Phoebe meets him, suitcase in hand, with firm plans to go with him. She persists in her demand to go until he changes his mind and decides to stay. Their close relationship, one of the few bright spots in Holden's life, literally saves him.

Once again, Kinsella's book echos the concerns and themes of *Catcher*, but it adds new twists. Like the other characters in the novel, Ray's brother Richard is also redeemed on Ray's farm. When Richard first comes to Iowa, he is unable to see the ghostly players or experience the magic of Ray's field. Toward the end of the novel, however, he begs Ray, "Teach me how to see" (239). His desire becomes even more heartfelt as he discovers that their father is one of the invisible players—the new catcher for the White Sox. Ray eventually realizes that the "he" of his first voice ("If you build it, he will come") refers both to Joe Jackson and to his father, John Kinsella. In an obvious pun on Salinger's title, Kinsella has Ray's father, a minor league baseball *catcher*, return from the dead to become the catcher in the corn. In the emotional climax of the novel the two sons finally work up the courage to approach their father. In a sudden epiphany Richard begins to see John, whom Ray consistently refers to as "the catcher":

> My father stops speaking and looks questioningly at Richard, who is squinting at him as though he is at the far end of a microscope.
>
> "He's been having a little trouble with his eyes, but I think it's clearing up," I say.
>
> "It's true," says Richard, air exploding from his lungs.
>
> "It's true," I reply.
>
> "I admire the way you catch a game of baseball," he says to the catcher, slowly, hesitantly, his voice filled with awe.
>
> As the three of us walk across the vast emerald lake that is the outfield, I think of all the things I'll want to talk to the catcher about.. I'll guide the conversations, like taking a car around a long, gentle curve in the road, and we'll

hardly realize that we're talking of love, and family, and life, and beauty, and friendship, and sharing. (255)

Both Richard and John are reborn on Ray's field, and the family relationships that had been permanently broken by death are magically restored.

The fact that Richard and Ray are brothers and Kinsella's inclusion of the carnival exhibit Richard owns—"the world's strangest babies"—suggests one final connection between *Shoeless Joe* and *Catcher in the Rye*. Holden visits two museums in the course of *Catcher*. The first, the Museum of Natural History, contains, among other things, dioramas of Native American life. Holden is most impressed by the seemingly immutable nature of the museum.

> The best thing, though, in that museum was that everything always stayed right where it was. Nobody'd move. You could go there a hundred thousand times, and that Eskimo would still be just finished catching those two fish, the birds would still be on their way south, the deers would still be drinking out of that water hole.... Nobody'd be different. The only thing that would be different would be *you*. (121)

At the second museum he visits, the Metropolitan Museum of Art, Holden, along with two young brothers, views a reconstruction of an Egyptian tomb. Here, once again, Holden notes a peaceful changelessness, explaining to the boys, "They wrapped their faces up in these cloths that were treated with some secret chemical. That way they could be buried in their tombs for thousands of years and their faces wouldn't rot or anything" (203). After the boys become scared and leave, Holden is left alone in the tomb. He notes, "I liked it, in a way. It was nice and peaceful" (204). Peter Shaw has pointed out that in both cases, Holden's museum experience "expresses his need for a moratorium on both death and love" (101). Holden yearns, literally, for the changeless peace of the tomb. Once again, though, he is denied what he seeks. The scrawled profanity in the tomb shocks him back to reality; not even the tomb is peaceful for Holden. He explains, "I think, even, if I ever die, and they stick me in a cemetery, and I have a tombstone and all, it'll say "Holden Caulfield" on it, and then what year I was born and what year I died, and then right under that it'll say 'Fuck you.' I'm positive, in fact" (204).

The tomb is certainly not a peaceful place for the players Ray helps in *Shoeless Joe*. Even in death, their yearning to fulfil their dreams continues to haunt them. Perhaps this is the core of Holden's complaint; death will not solve his problems either. Ray's field does not *suspend* love and death, but it does allow, if not the moratorium on death Shaw describes, then at least a reprieve, a chance to fulfil lost dreams. Richard's carnival trailer, on the other hand, filled with its glass cases and faded photographs, caricatures Salinger's museums and works as the antithesis of Ray's field. The attraction he owns, a pseudo-museum which claims to display "the world's strangest babies," is, in reality, a trailer with "about a dozen glass containers, like built-in fish tanks.... Each one contains a photograph of a deformed fetus and a small typed card describing the origins of the photo" (207–8). If Salinger's museums offer the illusion of a moratorium on death, Kinsella's "museum" suggests nothing of the kind. It puts death and decay on display and charges admission. Ray, like Holden, notes that the displays appear to have been unchanged for years, but in this case their changelessness suggests nothing so much as their total artificiality, their utter lack of life. "What did you expect," Richard's girlfriend demands, "live babies?" (208). Richard, caught in a twisted version of Holden's museum ideal, is redeemed only by Ray's renewed love and friendship and by the family ties he is able to reestablish with his father.[9] The words of the little boy Holden meets in the Met are particularly meaningful in the context of Richard and Ray's relationship: "He ain't my friend," the boy explains to Holden as his frightened sibling runs from the museum, "He's my brudda" (203).

The structure created by W. P. Kinsella in *Shoeless Joe* mirrors in surprising detail the pattern set by *Catcher in the Rye*. Kinsella, however, seems intent on *answering* the existential questions posed by the earlier novel. The world of Ray Kinsella is deeply meaningful, and it is, therefore, inherently different from the world of Holden Caulfield. In large measure,

Ray is able to fulfill Holden's dream of becoming a savior. For Ray, though, the rye has been transformed into corn, and the game being played in the field is baseball. Instead of keeping children from tumbling over a cliff, Ray offers salvation to adults who have lost their way in the world of spiritual shallowness and materialism. In Holden's world, a young boy can fall out of a dorm window to a meaningless death. In Ray's world, a young girl who falls off a bleacher can be miraculously saved by a ghostly doctor. In Holden's world, Allie's death is tragic—the end of friendship and family. In Ray's world, death is not final; family relations, love, and help can extend beyond the grave. Kinsella, in short, offers answers to Holden's problems that Salinger refused to offer. In *Shoeless Joe* Salinger's existential realism is replaced by Kinsella's magical realism.

One of Holden's most basic questions plagues all of us to some degree: how can life be meaningful in the face of a chaotic, violent, materialistic, and consumer-driven modern world? Helen Weinberg called *Catcher* "totally modern in its questions," and this is significant because she believes that in "the most honest modernist vision of the spiritual quest," the results can only be "inevitable failure" (66, 79).[10] Kinsella rejects this vision of the modern world and responds to Holden's failure with a sustained trope of redemption.[11] Ray eventually redeems even the fictional "Jerry" Salinger by offering him a world untainted by the kind of corruption which surrounds Holden. The fictional Salinger's "They will come"[12] oration near the end of *Shoeless Joe* has become one of the most famous speeches in contemporary pop culture. In a statement of born-again, secular faith, Salinger tells Ray that people will come to his small Midwestern farm to experience the peace he and the other characters have found there. "The arrivals will be couples who have withered and sickened of the contrived urgency of their lives," he explains.

> "They'll turn up in your driveway, not knowing for sure why they're doing it, and arrive at your door, innocent as children, longing for the gentility of the past, for home-canned preserves, ice cream made in a wooden freezer, gingham dresses, and black-and-silver stoves with high warming ovens and cast-iron reservoirs.

> "'Of course, we don't mind if you look around,' you'll say. 'It's only twenty
> dollars per person.' And they'll pass over the money without even looking at it—
> for it is money they have, and peace they lack." (252)

One of Salinger's final statements in the novel reaffirms this assurance, this
testimony of faith in the face of seeming chaos. When the players invite the
aging writer to return with them to the afterlife, he admits to Ray, "I
thought of turning them down.... But then I thought, they must know;
there must be a reason for them to choose me, just as there was a reason
for them to choose you, and Iowa, and this farm" (263). If *Catcher in the Rye*
is, as Gerald Rosen has suggested, a "novel of the death of belief in
America," then *Shoeless Joe* is about its potential rebirth and the possibility of
a post-postmodern renewal of faith (96).

NOTES

1. The literary battle Carol and Richard Ohmann and James E. Miller, Jr. have fought over
    Catcher may be understood at least in part as an expression of this polarization. The
    Ohmanns suggest a (Marxist) reading focused on Salinger's very real critique of society;
    Miller suggests a more personal reading with understanding Holden as the aim.

2. Like the fictional Ray Kinsella, W. P. Kinsella spent several years in Iowa (as part of the
    University of Iowa Writer's Workshop), and he calls Iowa "the only place I feel at
    home" (Dahlin 7). Kinsella did sell insurance before becoming a writer, and he does
    love baseball. His wife's name is Annie as is Ray's wife's name, and his father is John
    Kinsella, an ex-minor league player who died in 1953. Kinsella lived in Iowa for several
    years, and chased the baseball season in an old Datsun, as does Ray in the novel. The
    relationship between writer and character is close enough for Alan Cheuse to suggest
    that "Ray Kinsella, the novel's narrator, appears to be a doppelganger of the author
    himself" (V2).

3. See note number 7.

4. Phil Alden Robinson, a young Hollywood director, read the novel and found a story he
    believed would make a great film. Later he would note, "The only reason to adapt a

novel into a screenplay is because you love the novel" (*Field of Dreams; A Scrapbook*). He secured the rights, wrote a screenplay based on Kinsella's text, and received funding from Universal Pictures. When the real J. D. Salinger heard that the film was in preproduction, he had his lawyer contact Universal to warn them against using his name or likeness. Robinson was forced to rewrite Salinger's part, and, for the first time in his life, he wrote for a specific actor (*Field of Dreams; A Scrapbook*). It's probably not accidental that he chose James Earl Jones, an actor as different as possible from Salinger in appearance and temperament, to play the part. See Joseph Walker's essay in this collection for more discussion of the film.

5.   An obvious question here is why Salinger, known for his litigiousness, did not sue Kinsella and Random House for using his name and likeness. The answer has to do, ironically, with the writer's status as a public figure. He could not sue Kinsella for copyright violation, because Kinsella did not use any material that could be copyrighted (a book, letter, etc.). He may, however, have considered suing for character defamation. The traditional definition of defamation has three components: the statement in question must have been made to a third person (i.e., published in a novel); it must be untrue; and the victim must prove that harm was done. What Kinsella wrote in the novel was patently untrue, and Salinger could likely have claimed harm on the simple grounds of invasion of privacy. A landmark defamation case stood in his way, however. In 1964, a New York public official sued the *New York Times* for defamation (*NY Times vs. Sullivan*, 376 U S 1964). The case went all the way to the Supreme Court and was eventually decided in favor of the *Times*. The court decided that being a public official invites a greater degree of scrutiny. Officials, the court declared, had to prove actual malice on the part of the alleged defamer. In 1967, that notion was further broadened (*Curtis Publishing Company vs. Butts*, 388 US 1967) when the court found a strong correlation between public officials and other public figures. Salinger, as a public figure, would have to prove that Kinsella wrote the novel with malice, that is, that the Canadian author was out to get him. The deeply sympathetic portrayal of Salinger in the novel would suggest otherwise.

6.   In the novel, Ray confronts the fictional Salinger with an interview in which he claims to have wanted to play baseball for another New York team transplanted to California: the Giants (33–5).

7.   The "bankroll" for the fix was a well-known gambler named Arnold Rothstein, who put up $100,000 to pay off the players. Bluestein's name in the novel suggests that Kinsella was drawing a comparison between modern business and land development practices and illegal gambling. The author makes the connection more explicit when he later describes Bluestein as "wearing a wide-shouldered green corduroy suit that makes him look like a gangster" (241).

8. His mother and father, on the other hand, are conspicuous by their absence. Jonathan Baumbach suggests that one of Holden's main quests is for family and, specifically, for a father, someone who could guide his life. "The world," Baumbach argues, "devoid of good fathers…, becomes a soul-destroying chaos in which [Holden's] survival is possible only through withdrawal into childhood, into fantasy, into psychosis" (57).

9. An oddity of *Shoeless Joe* is that Ray and Richard's mother, though still living as the action takes place, is conspicuously absent. She is mentioned only once, briefly.

10. In her essay "Holden and Seymour and the Spiritual Activist Hero," Weinberg argues, in fact, that Salinger is not completely honest in *Catcher*, that he "cheats…on his own vision" by allowing Holden to succeed, at least partially, in his spiritual quest (64). She believes that Salinger's vision of the modern world is more honest in "Seymour: An Introduction."

11. In support of this idea, Kinsella said of his novel soon after publication, "I put in no sex, no violence, no obscenity, none of that stuff that sells. I wanted to write a book for imaginative readers, an affirmative statement about life" (Dahlin 7).

12. The line "They will come" is actually found only in *Field of Dreams*, the film version of *Shoeless Joe*.

WORKS CITED

Baumbach, Jonathan. "The Saint as a Young Man: A Reappraisal of 'The Catcher in the Rye'." *Critical Essays on Salinger's* The Catcher in the Rye. Ed. Joel Salzberg. Boston: G. K. Hall and Co., 1990. 55–63.

Cheuse, Alan. "An Outsider's Homage to Baseball Lore." *Los Angeles Times*, 23 May 1982: V2.

Dahlin, Robert. "W. P. Kinsella." *Publisher's Weekly* 221.16 (1982): 6–7.

"Dodger in the Rye." *Newsweek* 30 July 1979: 11–13.

Eppes, Betty. "What I Did Last Summer." *The Paris Review* 23.80 (1981): 221–239.

Field of Dreams. Dir. Phil Alden Robinson. Universal Pictures, 1989.

Field of Dreams; A Scrapbook. Banned from the Ranch Entertainment, 1990. (Promotional Video)

Fosburgh, Lacey. "J. D. Salinger Speaks About His Silence." *New York Times* 3 Nov. 1974: 1A.

Heiserman, Arthur, and James E. Miller, Jr. "J. D. Salinger: Some Crazy Cliff." *Critical Essays on Salinger's* The Catcher in the Rye. Ed. Joel Salzberg. Boston: G. K. Hall and Co., 1990. 32–39.

Horvath, Brooke and William Palmer. "Three On: An Interview with David Carkeet, Mark Harris, and W. P. Kinsella." *Modern Fiction Studies* 33, 183–194.

Kaplan, Charles. "Holden and Huck: The Odysseys of Youth." *The Catcher in the Rye.* Ed. Joel Salzberg. Boston: G. K. Hall and Co., 1990. 39–43.

Kinsella, W. P. *Shoeless Joe.* New York: Ballantine Books, 1982.

Miller, James. "'Catcher' In and Out of History." *Critical Essays on Salinger's* The Catcher in the Rye. Ed. Joel Salzberg. Boston: G. K. Hall and Co., 1990. 140–143.

Pearson, Ian. "Fantasy Strikes Out." Rev. of *Shoeless Joe. Macleans* 95.16 (1982): 59,61.

Plummer, William. "In Another League." Rev. of *Shoeless Joe. Newsweek* 23 Aug. 1982: 64.

Rosen, Gerald. "A Retrospective Look at 'The Catcher in the Rye'." *Critical Essays on Salinger's* The Catcher in the Rye. Ed. Joel Salzberg. Boston: G. K. Hall and Co., 1990. 158–171.

Rowe, Joyce. "Holden Caulfield and American Protest." *New Essays on* The Catcher in the Rye. Ed Jack Salzman. New York: Cambridge UP, 1991. 77–96.

Salinger, J. D. *The Catcher in the Rye.* Boston: Little Brown Books, 1951.

Salzman, Jack. Introduction. *New Essays on* The Catcher in the Rye. Ed. Jack Salzman. New York: Cambridge UP, 1991. 1–22.

Seelye, John. "Holden in the Museum." *New Essays on* The Catcher in the Rye. Ed. Jack Salzman. Cambridge: Cambridge UP, 1991. 23–34.

Shaw, Peter. "Love and Death in *The Catcher in the Rye.*" *New Essays on* The Catcher in the Rye. Ed. Jack Salzman. New York: Cambridge UP, 1991. 97–114.

Weinberg, Helen. "J. D. Salinger's Holden and Seymour and the Spiritual Activist Hero." *J. D. Salinger.* Ed. Harold Bloom. New York: Chelsea House Publishers, 1987. 63–80.

4.

The Catcher Takes the Field:
Holden, Hollywood, and the Making of a Mann

JOSEPH S. WALKER

> The goddam movies. They can ruin you. I'm
> not kidding.
> — Holden Caulfield

Texts do not, cannot, survive in utter isolation; characters, however compelling, do not speak to us across fifty years of vacuum. That J. D. Salinger's *The Catcher in the Rye* is vibrant and familiar to millions of readers half a century after its publication, particularly in a culture in which literacy in general and "Literature" in particular have lost much of their traditional privilege, is certainly in large part a testimony to the internal, self-contained virtues of the text itself. Primary among those virtues is Holden Caulfield, a character whose desperate, earnest sense of outraged decency remains compelling despite our growing distance from his colloquial speech and from the increasingly quaint social world of post-war Manhattan that plays host to his dissolution.[1] That said, however, *Catcher* also retains a significant presence in our cultural discourse by virtue of its place in a complex network of intertextual and even extratextual associations and affiliations. Like any piece of art that continues to hold our interest and claim relevance, the novel survives in part because of its manifestations in other expressive fields, its ability to grow beyond the borders of its own margins.

In the case of *Catcher*, it is the nonliterary ("real world") allusions and intersections that most conspicuously demand our attention, inevitably affecting our reading of the novel itself. We need hardly point again to the ironic juxtaposition of Holden's wish that authors he liked were "terrific friends" he could call on the phone with J. D. Salinger's own aggressive withdrawal from the public realm. The point is less that Salinger-as-hermit provides an invisible footnote to this particular passage than that his absence (which has become a kind of presence) by now pervades the entire text; it is the rare reader who can meditate on Holden's voice as an autonomous object distinct from the celebrated silence of his creator, likely read as another kind of response to a world all too liable to cause pain. Salinger's chosen silence, moreover, is balanced by the enforced silence embodied in the repeated attempts to remove *Catcher* from the shelves of schools and libraries, attempts which only ensure that the novel will continue to appear in the news and in anti-censorship campaigns on a regular basis. Can we read *Catcher* without some consciousness of these attempts at restriction, without noting their resonance with the various authorial figures within the novel attempting to bring Holden himself in line with the conventional—or with Holden's own desire to erase every "Fuck you" from every wall in New York? On an even more troubling level, can we listen to the voice of Holden—a self-proclaimed "pacifist" despite his frequent bursts of anger and annoyance—without some awareness of his reported ability to also speak to gunmen, assassins such as John Hinckley and Mark David Chapman? However absurd it is to implicate *Catcher* in their crimes, in their insanity, the fact that the novel has played prominently in their sensationalized media portraits is, if nothing else, indicative of the text's endlessly renewable aura of disruption; at least in mainstream culture, the book retains connotations of danger. For fifty years Holden Caulfield in his red hunting cap has been one face of teenage alienation and dissociation from societal norms, a kind of literary counterpart to James Dean in the famous red jacket. Given this, can we read Holden's joking about shooting people while wearing his hat (30) without hearing, however distantly, the echoes of Columbine?

I am not seeking here to implicate *The Catcher in the Rye*, J. D. Salinger, or even Holden Caulfield in crimes and conflicts that are clearly extraneous to the novel's composition and internal form. It is telling, however, that in our contemporary cultural field, *Catcher* is continually associated with moments and tendencies of disruption and tension, with violence, resistance, suppression, alienation and anxiety. Despite its apparently open surface, despite its frequent treatment as a children's book, despite even the relative neglect of a literary establishment which in many ways takes the book for granted, *Catcher* is repeatedly put in settings that remind us that it is ultimately a text of protest, a bitter critical barb aimed at the shallow pieties and casual cruelties still built into the daily functions of American life. If a coming-of-age story tells us how a child learns to assume an acceptable identity within a preexisting social realm, then Salinger's novel is the opposite of a coming-of-age story; it gives us a character who repeatedly rejects such prefabricated identities and smooth assimilation. Even at the end of the novel, after the epiphany that many critics have seen in the carrousel scene, Holden remains marginalized, ambivalent about the meaning of his experience and, crucially, still uncertain of what he is going to do next: "how do you know what you're going to do till you *do* it? The answer is you don't" (276). The properly socially conditioned subject, however, does know what he is going to do, if only because he is conscious of a limited set of options; but Holden remains unconditioned and essentially antagonistic to the dominant values his privileged upbringing was intended to have given him. It is tempting to see Salinger's own consciously chosen and zealously maintained isolation as the mature fulfillment of Holden's alienation, to see Salinger as the deaf-mute loner Holden fantasizes about becoming. Indeed, on some fundamental level, while this comparison is undoubtedly an oversimplification of the lived reality of Salinger's life and exactly the kind of overidentification with his work that is unfair to any artist, the fact remains that both Holden and Salinger reject both the conventional identities they could assume and the society which offers and structures those identities—and, furthermore, that that society finds such rejection, if not actively threatening, at least discomforting.[2]

Catcher, then, remains visible and viable in our contemporary cultural matrix in part through various nonliterary fields of negotiation that continue to highlight the novel's elements of resistance precisely through their efforts to neutralize them. But the text also survives through the more conventionally literary devices of allusion and reference, influence and revision. Even here, however, we may find that *Catcher*'s rough edges are smoothed over, its anger minimized, its disruptive potential lost. Specifically, I am interested in W. P. Kinsella's *Shoeless Joe* (1982)—a novel that, more explicitly than any other, consciously evokes both *The Catcher in the Rye* and J. D. Salinger himself—and in its film adaptation, Phil Alden Robinson's *Field of Dreams* (1989), which erases the most visible signs of Kinsella's references to Salinger but nonetheless remains a sort of bastard grandchild of Holden Caulfield.

As one of the most successful and visible films of the 1980s,[3] *Field*, despite the many changes it renders in Kinsella's narrative, has at least ensured that the basic premise of that narrative is widely familiar; thanks to the film, "If you build it, he will come" remains among the most recognizable pop culture catchphrases of the last two decades. Briefly, the novel is the first-person narrative of Ray Kinsella, an Iowa farmer who hears a mysterious voice telling him to plow under part of his corn in order to build a full-size baseball field. By following these instructions, Ray magically allows for the return of Shoeless Joe Jackson, the legendary Chicago White Sox left fielder who was forever barred from the game of baseball for throwing the 1919 World Series, and the other similarly disgraced "Black Sox," who use Ray's field to live out the ballgames they were never allowed to play in real life. The field and these games subsequently become the mechanisms for similar moments of redemption for a number of other characters, most prominently J. D. Salinger himself. In response to a second instruction from the voice—"ease his pain"—Ray tracks down Salinger in his New England retreat, forcing the reclusive author to attend a baseball game with him in Boston. There, Salinger receives his own mystic instructions, and from that point on he willingly accompanies Ray on his adventures, ultimately returning with him to Iowa. At the end of the novel, Salinger is invited by the ballplayers into the magical cornfield where they disappear between games, with the clear implication that he will be granted his boyhood dream of playing for the New York Giants at the Polo Grounds; he promises Ray, who has repeatedly lamented Salinger's decision to stop publishing, that he will write about the adventure. Immediately prior to this, Ray is granted his own wish that he has been working for throughout the narrative; he meets his father, dead many years, who has now been reborn as a young catcher living out his major league dream on his son's field (that Ray's father is a catcher rather neatly echoes the position of *The Catcher in the Rye* as the father-text of *Shoeless Joe*). For Ray, this reunion with his revitalized father, the man who gave him his fierce love of baseball, has been the goal from the beginning; the salvation he has delivered to Shoeless Joe and Salinger and the others has been secondary, a means to an end.

This uncritical valorization of and desire for the patriarch points to one of the significant differences between *Catcher* and *Joe*—one of the ways, in fact, in which the novels are actually in direct opposition—but before turning to these differences it is worth asking why Kinsella chooses Salinger for this role, what besides a coincidence of naming has drawn him to the author of *The Catcher in the Rye*. [4] A large part of the answer has nothing to do with Salinger's merits as an author or the internal characteristics of *Catcher* itself but with the fame and nostalgia generated by the novel and the entirely different kind of fame generated by Salinger's retreat from public life. That is to say, Salinger's cultural weight as expressed in *Joe* is largely—if not entirely—dependent upon the extratextual associations discussed above. From Kinsella's perspective, what Salinger apparently shares with someone like Shoeless Joe Jackson is the public accomplishment of something beautiful and entirely praiseworthy, followed by a descent into scandal and obscurity, a falling from grace. Don Murray, while perhaps excessive in his appreciation of Kinsella, accurately observes that *Joe*'s Salinger is a "diminished mountain king" and "ailing fertility figure ...who seems to have abdicated his sway over America's dreamland when he ceased publishing" (53). Such descriptions, I think, are more appropriate to Walt Disney than to the creator of Holden Caulfield, whose voyage through Manhattan is more akin to nightmare than to dream—but Ray, surely enough, tells Salinger that he wants to "renew" him, that the author must surely be "lonely" on his mountain. As they watch the Red Sox, he tells

Salinger of a sonnet he wrote to him while in college, "a plea to you to hurry and publish more stories." He says that Salinger's writing has "touched [his] soul," and that *The Catcher in the Rye* is "the definitive novel of a young man's growing pains" (82–85)—a reductive reading of *Catcher* that in many contexts would only be laughable.

Ray, in short, sees Salinger as the embodiment of the tortured artist, delivering through suffering and genius a work of unquestionable beauty and knowledge for the enlightenment of all, and believes that the author's life must be empty in the absence of such production and such reception. Salinger initially protests this idealized treatment ("'I don't know any answers,' he almost shouts" [83]), but by the end of the book, as he embraces the opportunity to return both to his youth and to writing, it becomes clear that he was simply being churlish. Indeed, before he even gets to Iowa, the world's most famous recluse is voluntarily revealing his identity to motel clerks and gas station attendants and is openly disappointed when they do not recognize his name or, worse, mistake him for Pierre Salinger or Truman Capote. Offered the chance to reclaim his public role, he almost immediately seizes it; the voice, after all, has declared that he is in pain in his exile, and so there is no use denying it. It is difficult to imagine a more romanticized, nostalgic, ultimately conservative view of the writer/artist—and equally difficult to imagine another contemporary American novelist on whom such a veil could rest, however lightly, however briefly. It is only Salinger's silence that allows Kinsella (allows the voice, allows Ray) to paint such a picture, to rewrite him in such a way. If Salinger's retreat can indeed be taken as a rejection of society—of the identity society forces writers into—then Kinsella essentially acts here to negate that rejection, to forcibly restore Salinger as the inspired oracle he has steadily refused to be. The voice might as well be Mr. Spencer, telling Salinger that he's only trying to put some sense into his head.

Where Salinger might reasonably and correctly object to this notion that his personal clock needs to be turned back,[5] it is a project that Holden, by contrast, might enthusiastically join in—and here, I think, we arrive at the fundamental thematic connection between the two novels, the logic of

Joe's forceful identification of *Catcher* as its textual father. Essentially, *Shoeless Joe* presents us with a sentimental, wish-fulfillment rendition of Holden Caulfield's most fervent desire: to stop—if not reverse—the passage of time. Holden's suffering, time and time again, results from his inability to accept or prevent change at some of its most basic levels. He is literature's most extreme preservationist, tormented by the fact that neither things nor people can be relied upon to stay the same, and for him their changes are universally associated with devolution; nothing in *Catcher* changes for the better. Most of Holden's truly traumatic moments occur when he perceives some threat to the innocence and authenticity he finds primarily in children; his premature flight from Pencey Prep, for example, is prompted in large part by his fight with Stradlater over the sexually aggressive boy's date with Jane Gallagher, the girl who kept all her kings in the back row when she and Holden had played checkers. This trait in itself is a telling image of preservation and stability, a privileging of potential, of the status quo, and of idiosyncratic pleasure ("'She just liked the way they looked'" [41]) at the expense of fully entering into the game, a game which is itself primarily a juvenile one, a preparation for the more warlike and adult pursuit of chess. It is particularly striking in light of Mr. Spencer's assertion, echoing Dr. Thurmer, that "'Life *is* a game, boy. Life *is* a game that one plays according to the rules'" (12). Jane's refusal to "play by the rules" marks her potential sympathy with Holden's fierce desire for the preservation of genuine youth, of innocence, of authenticity, and it is emblematic of his conflict with society as a whole that no one besides Holden finds any significance in her odd practice ("That kind of stuff doesn't interest most people" [41]). That Holden cannot bring himself to go speak to Jane, to find out if she still keeps her kings in the back row, points to his fear, to his dreadful knowledge that Jane, too, must inevitably change. That she might have changed so much as to "make time" with Stradlater, however, is unbearable beyond words or thoughts: "This next part I don't remember so hot," he confesses, just before describing his attack on Stradlater (56).

This is only one early manifestation of a pattern that recurs throughout the novel. Even when he is at his lowest points, an innocently happy child—the girl he helps with her skates, the boy who sings as he walks down the street—is enough to restore Holden: "It made me feel better. It made me feel not so depressed any more" (150). By contrast, a child in distress—the boy who cannot go to the bathroom because his mother is too engrossed in a film, the prostitute who is little more than a girl herself, Allie in his grave, unable to come in from the rain—can provoke his blackest moods and his deepest hatred of phonies. Thus the novel's title image: Holden as the guardian who allows the children to play safely, to stay away from danger—most prominently, the danger of adulthood. Ultimately it is his own childhood identity that is at stake here, slipping away despite his best efforts; recall his panic at the possibility that he might lose his virginity with Sunny, a panic that has less to do with performance anxiety than with the fact that, in a society devoid of formal rites of passage, sexual activity is all too frequently taken as a token of adulthood. To become an adult is to become a phony, to lose the purity and singularity of genuine identity. Holden's father is a lawyer, but Holden cannot imagine becoming one himself: "'Even if you *did* go around saving guys' lives and all, how would you know if you did it because you really *wanted* to save guys' lives, or because you did it because what you *really* wanted to do was be a terrific lawyer, with everybody slapping you on the back and congratulating you'" (223). Note that the fear here is not simply of being a phony but of being unsure whether you are a phony or not, of being alienated from true knowledge of yourself—much like Ernie, the piano player whose unexamined popularity has taken him to a place where "I don't even think he *knows* any more when he's playing right or not" (110). It is telling that Holden's father never appears in the novel (unlike his mother, whose voice is at least heard); he is kept offstage, perhaps because Holden is even less certain of his identity than that of D. B., the talented writer turned Hollywood prostitute. That *Shoeless Joe* so uncritically embraces the patriarchy that Holden cannot trust or approach (even to the extent of making Salinger himself something of a father figure for Ray) is ultimately one of the several ways in which the later novel works to redress the resistant aspects of the earlier.

It seems clear that Holden's anxiety over the inexorable press of change is made many times worse by the death of his idealized younger brother, Allie. While Holden is acutely aware of the tragedy of this death, Michael Cowan perceptively notes that he is also implicated in it: "By dying when he did, Allie never suffered that fall [into the phoniness of adulthood].... In order to preserve his image of Allie against the onslaughts of change, [Holden] has lovingly enshrined or 'mummified' Allie in his narrative and thus, strangely enough, become symbolically complicit in his death" (49). Ultimately, the only way to avoid change is to die, a possibility that Holden toys with at various points in his journey but cannot finally embrace. The end of the novel suggests that he prefers the alternative presented by Phoebe, his living younger sister, although he still must force himself to accept, even momentarily, the fact that he cannot protect or preserve her from growth and change: "The thing with kids is, if they want to grab for the gold ring, you have to let them do it" (273). Still, Allie remains a constant presence in the novel, a compact, multifaceted focal point of guilt, of unfulfilled potential balanced against the idealized embodiment of self, of the impossibility, from Holden's excessively sensitive perspective, of either living or dying. Crucially, although Holden speaks out loud to his brother several times as he grows weaker and more disoriented over the course of the novel, he is unable to dissociate the essential Allie from the material body that has been buried; as already noted, one of his darkest moments comes when he remembers it raining (*"twice"*) at the cemetery: "It rained on his lousy tombstone, and it rained on the grass on his stomach.... All the visitors could get in their cars and turn on their radios and all and then go someplace nice for dinner—everybody except Allie. I couldn't stand it" (202).

Without direct access to Allie himself, Holden is left with one potent material symbol of the boy: "My brother Allie had this left-handed fielder's mitt.... The thing that was descriptive about it, though, was that he had poems written all over the fingers and the pocket and everywhere. In green ink" (49). The use of "descriptive" in this passage is interesting; Holden seems to mean that the poems make the mitt a worthy subject for the essay he writes for Stradlater, but the actual construction of the sentence suggests that the mitt itself describes something else. Within the context of *Catcher*, that something can only be Allie. It is possible to see the essay Holden writes about the mitt (an essay which, clearly, is really about Allie himself) as his own version of that description, already implicit within the glove itself and to wonder whether the essay might not represent a potentially significant moment of healing for Holden, an opportunity for acceptance and restoration: "I sort of liked writing about it" (51). Writing, in this way, represents containment, coping, a way for Holden to finally come to terms with his loss by reclaiming Allie in a manageable form. This possibility is lost, however, when Stradlater angrily rejects the essay, and Holden, in a prelude to the fight over Jane and his flight from the school, seizes the pages and tears them up. Significantly, we never hear directly of the glove again after this; though Holden presumably packs it with his things before he leaves, it subsequently appears only in flashbacks. The destruction of the essay seems somehow to sever the direct link to Allie offered by the mitt, forcing Holden to experience his brother's loss all over again, and, coupled with the implied "loss" of Jane, it is simply too much.

If Holden's lost essay represents one textual expansion/revision of the already "descriptive" mitt, it is possible to see *Shoeless Joe* as another, the latter more sustained and totally given over to the conservative desire for preservation so central to Holden's character. It is a small step from a "left-handed fielder's mitt" to a legendary left fielder, a small step from poems written in green ink to Ray's insistently lyrical descriptions of baseball and of his field: "The left-field grass was like green angora, soft as a baby's cheek" (9). Wondering why Salinger (reinvented as a dedicated fan of the game by Kinsella) never wrote about baseball, Ray excitedly begins "bouncing up and down on [his] seat" when he abruptly remembers Allie's mitt, characteristically ignoring its primarily melancholy significance in order to see it as further evidence of his own connection to Salinger: "'*I* had a glove with green writing on it when I was a kid'" (86–87). Interestingly, Ray misidentifies Allie's mitt as a "left-fielder's glove," a mistake which allows him to tie Shoeless Joe directly into the symbol as well, completing his trinity. Are we to see Ray, then, as an adult version of Allie? Such a reading is entirely in keeping with the overall pattern of Kinsella's novel, a pattern in which time and all its negative effects—loss, pain, dissolution, phoniness—are magically rendered nonexistent. Why should Allie's death matter any more, in such a narrative, than those of Shoeless Joe, of Ray's father, of any of the dozens of other characters who are returned to life by Ray Kinsella's ballpark?

Nor is it only death that ceases to have meaning in the "dream currency" of Iowa's "precious land" (5). Before Shoeless Joe arrives, Ray resolves that he will not sully the moment by asking him about the truth of the charges against him (9). In the event, however, he does ask—not about the crime, but about the expulsion from the game and how it felt. Joe's answer ("'Years and years later, I'd wake in the night with the smell of the ballpark in my nose and the cool of the grass on my feet'" [14]) is one of the book's many romanticized tributes to the game itself, but he speaks entirely of the pain of losing contact with it, essentially implying that the reason for that loss is random, an unmotivated accident. Even after the other banned players (many of whom, unlike, Joe were guilty beyond a doubt) join him, the 1919 World Series itself never truly becomes an issue in the book. Not only are none of the players ever confronted with the question of their guilt, but they are all, like Joe, invested with the pure love of the game that every sympathetic character in the novel shares and that surely renders such a violation unthinkable. Time, in other words, has not merely been reversed; it has been erased. Holden's dislike of phoniness could hardly find a more apt target than a baseball player who only pretends to try to win, but that phoniness and corruption, for all intents and purposes, never exist in Kinsella's world. The Black Sox are reinvented here, as pure and unsullied as Allie himself; as with Allie, it has become inconceivable that they have fallen or could ever fall.

Similar erasures occur throughout the novel. Eddie Scissons, who owned Ray's farm before him and who had claimed to be the oldest living Chicago Cub, is eventually revealed to be a sham who never really had a major league career. Ray's brother-in-law Mark, the cartoonishly evil landowner trying to drive Ray off his property and destroy the field, suggests this is the ultimate betrayal: "'You claim to know so much about baseball, claim it's so pure and wonderful. How can you let him worm his way into your game?'" Ray, however, has no hesitation: "I wonder how I can. But I know I can. Fact and fantasy swirl together" (218). In fact, forgiveness is never truly an issue, for within the magical sphere of Ray's game, no transgression severe enough to cause lasting damage can happen; no fact can stand against the dominant force of lived fantasy. Shortly after this exchange, Eddie does in fact see his younger self trot on to Ray's field and pitch against the White Sox, in some way fulfilling the story he has told for years, negating his own phoniness. Though he watches himself perform miserably, Eddie is only confirmed in his belief in the game; make love of the game your common ground, he tells Ray, "'and nothing else will matter'" (230). In Ray's Garden, it would seem, it is never too late for the apple to be put back on the tree.

However perfectly this fulfils Holden's most obsessive desires, *Catcher* itself in no way endorses or accepts this idea that change can be negated, that phoniness can be neutralized, that life's finest moments, like museum exhibits, can be indefinitely preserved under glass. The critical debate over whether Holden ever realizes and accepts this—Can we see his return to his family and his willingness to allow Phoebe to take risks on the carrousel as indicating a new acceptance of what is demanded of him? Does the institutional setting of the brief final chapter indicate a relapse?—stretches back almost to the beginning of critical assessment of the novel. Personally, I see Holden, in the last pages of the book, as succumbing to the final stages of exhaustion rather than coming to a new understanding of life. Then again, I see no real need in him for a *new* understanding; I think that Holden knows from very early on his quest to protect innocence is doomed, but that even to the very end he cannot bring himself to abandon it. What seems beyond debate is that the form of the novel itself demonstrates both the impossibility and the unhealthiness of attempting to actually *be* a catcher in the rye, of trying to preserve everything that is pure. This is not to suggest that Salinger endorses those corruptive aspects of society which alienate and frighten Holden—the casual arrogance of Stradlater, the violent dishonesty of Maurice, the neglect of children, the divisive snobbery of his schools. Rather, it is merely to note that these destructive forces cannot ultimately be defeated or even avoided; to insist they can be, as *Shoeless Joe* does, is to neuter both *Catcher* and Salinger, to reframe a potent voice of protest as little more than the misguided grumble of a pessimist. If we play Ray's game, *Joe* tells us, we will never again have to fear or lose anything. Though he would like to believe it, Holden knows better: "If you get on the side where all the hot-shots are, then it's a game, all right—I'll admit that. But if you get on the *other* side, where there aren't any hot-shots, then what's a game about it? Nothing. No game" (12–13).

That said, every text has its shadowy counter-text, its internal moments of disruption and hesitation, and *Shoeless Joe* is no exception; for all its lyrical celebration of endless renewal, it is strangely haunted by a handful of oddly dark moments, most of them involving the children Holden so desperately wishes to save. Before they attend their game in Boston, for example, Ray and Salinger eat at a Greek restaurant down the street from the park. There, they are approached by "a small boy about tabletop height" who happily inserts himself into their conversation, telling them that he has had a piece of strawberry pie. As the two men "prepare to leave, the boy skips along" with them; the proprietor assumes he is theirs and tells them that the boy has been simply wandering around the restaurant for an hour. Denying any connection, Ray says the child is too healthy and well dressed to have been abandoned, and as he and Salinger leave "the boy is staring after me as if I'd just kicked his cat" (79–80). The boy is never mentioned again, and he plays no readily identifiable part in the symbolic structure of the novel; possible explanations (Is he somehow Ray's father, reborn but too young yet for the field?) are little more than encoded confusion. The boy's obviously hurt feelings, coupled with Ray's and Salinger's ability to simply walk away from him without a second thought, stand as a troubling oddity, a nettlesome burr in the middle of the text. He is, at the simplest level, a child who is not being cared for; as such, he represents, however briefly, the darkness that *Catcher* obsessively registers and *Joe* so strenuously ignores.

This function is still more apparent in a macabre display later in the novel. In another subplot of renewal, too complex to fully explore here, Ray is reunited with his long-lost identical twin brother, Richard, who has become a carnival barker. Late in the novel, Ray views the sordid interior of a trailer where Richard sings out a spiel inviting carnival attendees to see the "strange babies": "about a dozen glass containers, like built-in fish tanks, are inset at intervals. Each one contains a photograph of a deformed fetus and a small typed card describing the origins of the photo, with a few clinical details" (207–208). Although it is possible to see this display as an indication of the troubled life from which Richard must be rescued (among the sympathetic characters, only Richard, at least initially, cannot see the supernatural manifestations on Ray's field), its grotesque presence in the novel stands as an unanticipated vision of childhood utterly corrupted and destroyed—and displayed, for good measure, in a cynical bid for profit. Like the mysterious boy in Boston, the exhibit stands as an anomalous mark, a disturbing residue of the more troubling aspects of *Joe*'s parent text.

It hardly needs to be said that neither of these scenes survives into *Field of Dreams*. Of course, the film must—if only because of time restrictions—streamline *Shoeless Joe* considerably, eliminating a series of significant subplots and characters such as Eddie and Richard.[6] Even the aspects of the novel that are retained, however, are altered in ways that further deepen their conservative, don't-worry-be-happy message. For our purposes, the most significant of these changes is the alteration of J. D. Salinger into a character who shares most of his plot functions but relatively few of his characteristics: James Earl Jones's Terence Mann. As already noted, the decision not to use "Salinger" in the film was, for all practical purposes, a legal necessity, but it is the particular form his replacement takes that interests me here. Struggling to design a suitable character to assume Salinger's role, Phil Alden Robinson decided that it would be fun to see Ray Kinsella compelled to kidnap "a really big guy" and thus wrote the role of Mann specifically for Jones.[7] While Jones's size and his character's considerable initial hostility do make Mann's first encounter with Ray more dynamic than Salinger's (in the novel Salinger is initially presented as extremely defensive and suspicious but also somewhat passive), this casting also introduces an African-American presence into the relationship and into the narrative.

In Kinsella's novel, the presence of African Americans is limited to a few background extras, either frightening or pathetic, glimpsed in big, decaying cities. (Caroline M. Cooper and other critics have, quite properly, called Kinsella to task for this problematic treatment.) The casting of Jones in one of the film's most central roles, however, apparently necessitates a more direct (if not necessarily more enlightened) treatment of racial identity and politics. Mann, therefore, is not simply a fondly remembered writer who has stopped publishing and whose books are sometimes banned; he is a former radical activist, an advocate of black power whose works are strongly identified with the social upheavals of the sixties: "The man wrote the best books of his generation," Ray, clad in a Berkeley T-shirt, tells his wife Annie. "He was a pioneer in the civil rights and the antiwar movements…. He helped shape his time. I mean, the guy hung out with the Beatles." Annie herself, at a school board meeting where Mann is denounced for promoting (among other things) "the mongrelization of the races and disrespect to high-ranking officers of the United States Army," credits her "favorite writer" for coining the phrase "Make love, not war." Even Mann's reasons for abandoning publishing have more to do with the very public struggles of the time than a desire for privacy; he tells Ray that he gave up being "involved" when "they killed Martin and Bobby, [and] they elected Tricky Dick twice—and now people like you think I must be miserable because I'm not involved any more." To a certain extent these associations are necessary to lend Mann at least a portion of the cultural significance that J. D. Salinger possesses by virtue of his very name. That they further represent a fundamental shift between the two characters, however, is indicated by the respective titles of their books: *The Catcher in the Rye* draws its title from Holden's fantasy of preservation and maintenance, while Mann's most famous title—*The Boat Rocker*—points to agitation, disruption, rebellion.

Of course, Salinger cannot be wholly dissociated from the disruptions of the sixties, though he himself had stopped publishing by the middle of the decade. John Seelye argues that Holden's voice, which mostly fell on deaf ears in the self-satisfied fifties, found its true audience in the following decade: "It was definitely the Boy in the Red Hunting (i.e., Liberty) Cap who led the rest of the literary pack in arousing a nation of kids to a higher consciousness of universal fraud, acting as a transcendental Special Prosecutor of Adult Values and making straight the way for the protest movements" (24). But while Holden may have influenced the open, aggressive resistance now collectively signified by the very label "the sixties," his own characteristic tactics of resistance are isolated withdrawal and critical observation rather than confrontation and collective protest— and of course, Salinger himself played little if any public role in any of the movements with which Mann is so forcefully identified. We might well see Mann, then, as the active, noisy fulfillment of the passive, quiet potential for resistance that Holden embodies—a fulfillment made necessary by Jones's race (Is it conceivable that a black writer of the period could have achieved fame outside the framework of the contemporary movements?), by the need to give his character an identity that would be immediately meaningful to the audience, and, finally, by the simple fact that *Joe* is set in the late seventies while *Field* is set in the late eighties, effectively moving the entire backstory forward by a decade.

Indeed, this simple time shift is largely responsible for the fact that the sixties—which are barely mentioned in Kinsella's novel—are a significant presence throughout much of the film. Ultimately, however, the film's treatment of this material—and, thus, of Mann—is deeply troubling, extending even the conservatism embedded in *Joe*. Although Ray and Mann both pay lip service to the ideals that motivated the activism of the sixties, they also participate in the film's persistent discrediting and disavowal of those same ideals. This begins to become apparent in the very first sequence of the film, a montage of still photographs and stock footage over which Ray narrates a history of his family from the birth of his father to the present. This significantly alters the story as told in the novel[8]; where

Kinsella's Ray lived harmoniously with his father through a shared love of baseball until the very moment of the older man's death, the film assigns to Ray the hostile and antagonistic relationship that his father originally had with Kinsella's now-vanished Richard (much later in the film, Ray tells Mann—to the author's disgust—that their final argument was touched off by Ray's reading of *The Boat Rocker*). Ray, in fact, deliberately escalates their battle by choosing to go to college at Berkeley, where "officially my major was English, but really it was the sixties. I marched, I smoked some grass, I tried to like sitar music, and I met Annie." This narration—which, like Ray's declaration that Mann "hung out with the Beatles," is deliberately dismissive of the serious issues at stake in sixties cultural activism—is matched to period footage of hippies dancing in a park and marching, but the underlying intent of the sequence is clear. On the film's commentary track, Robinson happily recalls watching audience members, who were initially uncertain of the nature of the film in its early screenings: "when that sixties footage comes up, I remember people really laughing…they knew how to react to that."

This laughter is deliberately evoked in the body of the film as well. When Ray quotes a passage from one of Mann's books to him in their first meeting, the author cries "Oh, my God, you're from the sixties" and begins to spray him with insecticide; in response to Ray's disappointed realization that "you've changed," Mann makes a peace sign and bellows "Peace, love, dope!" The dismissive laughter, though, is less damaging than the primary function of the sixties in the plot: they are the wedge that drove Ray and his father apart, through Ray's merely conformist adherence to what the film clearly regards as dangerous and/or silly ideas. Where Kinsella's Ray seeks reunion with his father merely out of familial love, the film's Ray must use his magical field to redeem himself for a transgression as unimaginable as Shoeless Joe's own: having been "an American boy refusing to have a catch with his father." The book's freely given gesture of love and belief becomes, in the film, what Mann refers to as Ray's "penance."

The film's central ideological project, then, is to erase the sixties; to correct the errors wrought by a wide set of social movements that dared, figuratively and literally, to oppose the patriarch; to silence the "misguided" children who spoke, at least in part, in Holden Caulfield's voice. The absurdity of this becomes apparent in the closing minutes of the film, when Mann stands before the bleachers and delivers, to Ray and a handful of other listeners, a poetic tribute (excerpted from a much longer version, delivered in *Joe* by Salinger) to the glory of baseball, and specifically to its power to "remind us of all that was good, and that could be again." The game, he says, has been "the one constant through all the years" even as America has been "erased like a blackboard, rebuilt and erased again." Baseball, in other words, can take us all back to a time before things became so chaotic—to a time before the sixties, before, ironically, Terence Mann himself. The speech is excessive enough in its sentimentality in the novel; what brings it to the very limit of reactionary fantasy in the film is the sight of the players on the field who gather behind Mann to listen to him. They are, of course, major league baseball players from the first decades of the twentieth century—and they are, of course, all white. Standing before them, speaking for them, Mann, despite a reference earlier in the film to his boyhood desire to play with "Jackie Robinson and the Brooklyn Dodgers" and despite his own status as one of the men who has attempted to erase and rebuild America, is made to speak nostalgically of his own subjugation and to apologize, however obliquely, for the damage he has wrought in seeking to end it. Whatever fondness the characters or we may genuinely feel for baseball, to proffer this excessively nostalgic, blindingly homogenous version of it as an idealized balm for the pain of America is, in the deepest sense, phony.

None of this, I think, can be very surprising to readers of *The Catcher in the Rye*; certainly little of it would be surprising to Holden. *Field of Dreams*, after all, merely confirms his deep-seated suspicion of Hollywood; in the very first paragraph of his book he tells us that "If there's one thing I hate, it's the movies" (4). The self-conscious performativity of Mann's speech is ultimately of a piece with the stylized, artificial self-satisfaction Holden objects to not only in Ernie but in Olivier, in the Lunts, and in all of the films he mentions in the course of his story. His antipathy, perhaps, is not entirely unconnected to the fact that he feels the pull of the movies; for someone who professes to hate them, he certainly brings them up frequently. Moreover, they provide the stuff of his imagination, of his tentative play with identity. Watching Stradlater shave, he "started imitating one of those guys in the movies. In one of those *musicals*. I hate the movies like poison, but I get a bang imitating them" (38). Punched in the stomach by Maurice, he "started pretending I had a bullet in my guts. Old Maurice had plugged me. Now I was on the way to the bathroom to get a good shot of bourbon or something to steady my nerves and help me *really* go into action" (135–136). For Holden, the movies are a seductive but corruptive source of prefabricated speech, identity, and action, the very antithesis of his idealistic quest for the authentic. The movies are always already phony, and they force him to confront the phoniness within himself—namely, his denial of, or resistance to, the fact that he has already lost his battle for the preservation of innocence. *Field of Dreams*, ultimately, merely deepens the particular phoniness already present in *Shoeless Joe*, as, like Mann, the ghosts of Salinger, *Catcher*, and Holden are brought forward in both these texts and made to speak in defense of an idealized vision of America that has no room for their doubts, their anger, their rejection; in short, they are made to repent for ever questioning Father. The fact that *Joe* and *Field* do violence to their own textual father(s) in this process is, we can only assume, overlooked or dismissed as insignificant.

NOTES

1.   Indeed, Holden's voice so dominates the novel that it may be partly responsible for the relative dearth of serious criticism of *Catcher*. Salinger's supreme creation is not the novel but the character; it is Holden we remember and carry with us, so much so that many critics of the novel devote their energy to demonstrating that it (and, therefore, Salinger) does not fully endorse his perceptions and conclusions. Anticipating Kinsella,

such readings license Salinger to cry out that he is *not* Holden Caulfield (*Joe* 87). We might draw a tentative connection here between Salinger and later "domestic" writers such as Raymond Carver and Bobbie Ann Mason, whose seemingly exclusive focus on the personal and the subjective can seem out of step with the sprawling multimedia world that has become the primary object of interest for contemporary theory. In this setting it becomes all too easy to leave *Catcher* in the high schools, to see it as simply a story of adolescence for adolescents.

2. Another expression of this discomfort is the publication, within the last few years, of memoirs by a former lover of Salinger's and by his daughter. Even setting aside their content (both authors make bizarre allegations about Salinger's life, habits, and beliefs), such volumes are, by their very existence, attacks upon Salinger's readily apparent desire for privacy and solitude, attempts to force him into roles he does not wish to take. In a documentary on the making of the film *Field of Dreams* (available on the DVD of the film itself), W. P. Kinsella says that he chose to use Salinger in *Shoeless Joe* out of an interest in how Salinger has made himself "conspicuous by hiding." This basic attitude—that because Salinger hides, we somehow have the right to seek him— essentially insists upon forging a relationship where none need exist, putting us in the position of multiple public Spencers chiding Salinger for his inappropriate behavior.

3. For a discussion of how *Field of Dreams* participates in the conservative impulses of Reaganite film—a discussion to which I am indebted here—see Alan Nadel's excellent *Flatlining on the Field of Dreams.*

4. As is noted within *Shoeless Joe*, there is in fact a character named "Ray Kinsella" in Salinger's short story "A Young Girl in 1941 with No Waist at All." In *Catcher*, Holden tells Mr. Antolini about a classmate named Richard Kinsella; *Joe* gives this name, as we will see, to Ray's twin brother. For a fuller exploration of the significance of these intertextual names, see Dennis Cutchins's essay in this volume.

5. Indeed, by Kinsella's own account the manuscript of *Shoeless Joe* was met with "a letter from Salinger's lawyers, a grumbling letter stating that J. D. was outraged and offended to be portrayed in my novel and that they would be very unhappy if it were transferred to other media." Thus Salinger was replaced in *Field of Dreams* by Terence Mann (Murray 49). The familiar "J. D." and the condescension of "grumbling" here smack of precisely the kind of presumption Salinger is objecting to.

6. A final note on the differences between Salinger and Kinsella: where Salinger has steadfastly refused to allow any filmed version of *Catcher*, Kinsella turned over *Joe* with only a sense that "I would be disappointed if they made a dreadful teenage movie out of it—'Shoeless Joe Meets Rocky VI'—but their money entitles them to do whatever they please" (Murray 49).

7. My discussion of the making of *Field of Dreams* derives largely from the commentary track and documentary available on the current DVD of the film.

8. Among the other changes, Ray's mother—still alive in the novel—dies when he is three in the film, leaving Ray's father to raise him alone. This, of course, deepens the veneration of the patriarch already present in the novel; "the mother's nurturing function has been almost immediately appropriated by the father, an appropriation that is consistently evidenced in American films upholding a patriarchal ideology" (Kirtz 29).

WORKS CITED

Cooper, Caroline M. "*Field of Dreams*: A Favorite of President Clinton—But a Typical Reaganite Film?" *Literature-Film Quarterly* 23(3): 163–68.

Cowan, Michael. "Holden's Museum Pieces: Narrator and Nominal Audience in *The Catcher in the Rye*." *New Essays on* The Catcher in the Rye. Ed. Jack Salzman. Cambridge: Cambridge UP, 1991. 35–56.

Field of Dreams. Screenplay and direction by Phil Alden Robinson. Universal, 1989.

Kinsella, W. P. *Shoeless Joe*. Boston: Houghton Mifflin, 1982.

Kirtz, Mary K. "Canadian Book, American Film: *Shoeless Joe* Transfigured on a *Field of Dreams*." *Literature-Film Quarterly* 23(1): 26–31.

Murray, Don. *The Fiction of W. P. Kinsella: Tall Tales in Various Voices*. Fredericton: York Press, 1987.

Nadel, Alan. *Flatlining on the Field of Dreams: Cultural Narratives in the Films of President Reagan's America*. New Brunswick: Rutgers UP, 1997.

Salinger, J. D. *The Catcher in the Rye*. Boston: Little, Brown, 1951.

Seelye, John. "Holden in the Museum." *New Essays on* The Catcher in the Rye. Ed. Jack Salzman. Cambridge: Cambridge UP, 1991. 23–34.

5.

Love, Loss, and Growing Up in
J. D. Salinger and Cormac McCarthy

MATT EVERTSON

> I'd rather have a goddam horse. A horse is at
> least *human*, for God's sake.
> — Holden Caulfield, 16
> *The Catcher in the Rye*

> What he loved in horses was what he loved in
> men, the blood and the heat of the blood that
> ran them.
> — John Grady Cole, 16
> *All the Pretty Horses*

Shortly after its publication in 1951, critics began comparing the *Catcher in the Rye*, for better or worse, to one of the most important and influential works in the American canon: *Adventures of Huckleberry Finn*. Fifty years later, *The Catcher in the Rye* has become the lodestone to which much contemporary adolescent fiction now points. In the tradition of comparing Holden to Huck, I would argue that the best contemporary candidate to pick up the mantle of *The Catcher in the Rye*—a work that captures the adolescent thrill of running away, the fear of growing up and leaving home, and which lays bare the complex angst of love and death in the lives of young people—is Cormac McCarthy's *All the Pretty Horses*. While little is documented about the influence J. D. Salinger has had on Cormac McCarthy (himself very reclusive, not given to interviews), there are undeniable similarities between each writer's most popular work.[1] *The Catcher in the Rye* was written and takes place in the late 1940s, while *All the*

Pretty Horses was published in 1992 but takes place in 1949. McCarthy details the Southwestern and Mexican adventures of sixteen-year-old John Grady Cole during the same period that Holden Caulfield (also sixteen) struggles through his mental and physical collapse in an East Coast metropolis. The titles of both works reference songs of children: a skewed version of the Robert Burns poem sung by a boy on a Sunday morning sidewalk ("If a body *catch* a body coming through the rye") and a traditional children's lullaby ("All the Pretty Little Horses").[2] And while a New Yorker and a Texan might seem to have little in common, Holden Caulfield and John Grady Cole both fantasize about reclaiming a romantic West and escaping the materialistic and selfish adult society that has abandoned them. Even horses mark time in both novels, as the epigraphs above indicate, riding at the core of John Grady's universe (allowing his escape from the oil-boon snags of fresh Texas highways and fencelines) and sidling into city-boy Holden's fantasies of flight, a more "human" answer to the coarse mechanics of Ed Banky's car (especially, its back seat). Both novels offer a dead-aim analysis of the universal condition of growing up, concentrated on the very threshold between the child and adult—with its movement, escape, borders, and barriers on two distinct geographical landscapes and from two distinct historical vantage points—in the same period of what some consider America's own tumultuous "coming of age" (her economic, political, and artistic growth following World War II).

While few, if any, critics have drawn this comparison—and admittedly far removed from the halls of Pencey Prep and the streets of Manhattan— McCarthy's novel, like *The Catcher in the Rye*, has become a favorite in advanced high school classrooms and can be seen lining the assigned reading shelf of many a college bookstore. Why do young readers embrace such works? What is the formula for success? After all, the compelling world of Holden Caulfield was created by a 30-year-old combat veteran. How could McCarthy successfully visit the adolescence of John Grady Cole when he himself was in his late fifties (and is the author of a notoriously gory classic of American Western settlement, *Blood Meridian*, which Harold Bloom places in the same league of literary high-seriousness as *Moby Dick*).

Today many readers young and old—few having attended a prep school in the age of Eisenhower—are still deeply affected by Holden Caulfield and his disturbing adventures, just as legions of readers continue to drift with Huck down the troubled river of antebellum America. Leslie Fiedler, writing during the first wide reappraisal of Salinger in the late 50s and early 60s, attempted to explain the enduring impact of adolescent works like *Huck Finn*. Why, he asked in *Love and Death in the American Novel*, do American writers so often craft characters fleeing to the wilderness, seeking adolescent adventure, fumbling with mature heterosexual love, escaping the conflicts of adult society—issues contemplated in Twain, Salinger (and, now, McCarthy)? Fiedler argues that *The Catcher in the Rye* compares more favorably to the sentimentality of *Tom Sawyer* than to the tragic and classic consequence of *Huck Finn,* but one point of his analysis is particularly relevant to unlocking the enduring and powerful appeal of such works: "If *Huckleberry Finn* is, finally, the greatest of all books about childhood," Fiedler argues, "this is because it renders with a child's tough-mindedness and a child's desperate hilarity a double truth fumbled by most other books on the subject: how truly wonderful it is to remember our childhood; and yet how we cannot recall it without revealing to ourselves the roots of the very terror, which in adulthood has driven us nostalgically to evoke that past" (289).

By taking a closer look at Salinger, through a comparison to McCarthy, perhaps we can uncover how these mature, world-weary men writing about young boys have so effectively captured—as Fiedler puts it—both the nostalgia of childhood and the "roots of the very terror" that growing up signifies. More specifically, the universal and continuing appeal of *The Catcher in the Rye* and the newfound success of that formula in *All the Pretty Horses,* I believe, can be traced to three primary issues that resonate powerfully with teenagers—when they first pick up the books—and with adult readers when they return to them in nostalgia. First is a focus on the choice and control that young adults yearn for in their lives, of making their own unique path into an adult world they feel is corrupt or has failed them in various ways. Second are compelling explorations of innocence and youth and the ability or inability to control the processes of time and maturation; these stories and characters frankly address the unspoken fears of growing up, appealing to young readers who, although unlikely to admit it, fret deeply over the transition from familiar childhood to the uncertainty of adulthood and social responsibility that awaits . Finally, the controlling themes of love and death elevate these works into the American canon; for many young readers, these adventures may be the first serious confrontations with the weighty issues of mortality, sexuality, belief, faith, love, and loss.

Taking Control and Taking Off

> I put my red hunting hat on, and turned the peak around to the back, the way I liked it, and then I yelled at the top of my goddam voice, "Sleep tight, ya morons!"
> — *The Catcher in the Rye*

> If I dont go will you go anyways?
> John Grady sat up and put his hat on. I'm already gone, he said.
> — *All the Pretty Horses*

Both *The Catcher in the Rye* and *All the Pretty Horses* begin with escape. In the thrill of running away, however, one forgets that John Grady Cole and Holden Caulfield are homeless, both physically and emotionally, and that sixteen-year-olds wandering the deserted streets at night, be it in Manhattan or Mexico, is in fact a sad circumstance. Forced to take off on their own, these characters remind us of their abandonment—no nurturing parents to embrace them with comforting arms, no reasonable adults to hear their needs and provide for their emotional well-being.

Though born into a life of privilege, Holden hints in the opening pages an emotional poverty in his family life even while refusing to discuss his "lousy childhood" or how his parents were "occupied" before they had him and all the "David Copperfield kind of crap" (3). One of the more powerful images of Holden's isolation is prominently featured in these opening pages, when the reader joins a solitary boy standing on top of Thompson Hill, who has been ostracized for losing the fencing team's gear in the city, looking down upon generations of the "Pencey family" gathered for the traditional football rivalry with Saxon Hall: "you could hear them all yelling, deep and terrific on the Pencey side, because practically the whole school except me was there" (5). Despite the blasé attitude he affects, the scene stresses that Holden at sixteen is a practiced outsider, having already faced a lifetime of upheavals, moved around like one of the checkers he speaks of so reverently in regard to Jane Gallagher (no wonder he admires her impulse to keep her kings safely and predictably at home in the back row). Hanging around for "some kind of a good-by," Holden expresses a desire to control his exile, to stage his exit, and to take his leave on his own terms. "I don't care if it's a sad good-by or a bad good-by," he argues, "but when I leave a place I like to *know* I'm leaving it. If you don't, you feel even worse" (7). When his bloody confrontation with Stradlater hastens his flight, his parting shot to his "moron" prep school companions recasts Holden as misunderstood victim, willing to face a cold night without sure shelter while they insensitively "sleep tight" in their collusion against him. His "decision" to leave, then, subverts the plan to kick him out, delays what can only be an unpleasant return to his parents, and buys him (along with the proceeds of his hawked typewriter) a couple of days on his own in the city.

Despite his posturing towards independence, when Holden first arrives in New York he "accidentally" gives the cab driver the address of his parent's apartment betraying, many critics theorize, his true desire to retreat to his boyhood "home" rather than to hit the town. If he longs to be "welcomed" home, the inevitable anger and disappointment of his parents and the attendant loss of his control and independence keep him on the run. Instead, Holden will try to construct a home built towards his own comfort and control; his sparse and lonely hotel room, however, proves a poor domestic space, and the denizens of New York night life provide little in the way of "family." Finding little companionship with the three young women tourists in the hotel lounge, Holden hails a cab to Greenwich Village. Trying to draw the cabby, Horwitz, into a friendly conversation, he asks if he knows where the ducks in Central Park go in the winter. Horwitz, however, dismisses Holden and argues that the fish in the frozen lake are of more concern than the "stupid" ducks. Joining a long list of incredulous spectators to Holden's attempts to pass as an adult, Horwitz asks "How the hell old are you, anyways?" and "Why ain'tcha home in bed?" (109). Later in the novel a drunk and obnoxious Holden confronts the piano player in the bathroom of the Wicker Bar, who urges him to "Go home, Mac, like a good guy. Go home and hit the sack." An intoxicated Holden reveals the hard truth: "No home to go to. No kidding" (198). When he finally leaves the bathroom, he's crying and "feeling so damn depressed and lonesome" (198). He then wanders to an abandoned Central Park, to the pond, looking for those ducks. Perhaps they remind him of his own desire to take flight, the consequence of leaving home, or the inability to find permanence and comfort. Or perhaps Horwitz was onto something: Holden is like a fish out of water on the streets of New York, alone and—by the end of the novel— seemingly gasping for air each step he takes. Yet the frozen lake, home by nature to the fish, is also incapacitating, harsh, and enclosed. "If you was a fish, Mother Nature'd take care of *you*, wouldn't she?" Horwitz argues. "You don't think them fish just *die* when it gets to be winter, do ya?" (109). Like many a teenager, Holden confronts the question of who *will* take care of him as he matures, trapped between the frightening freedom of being alone and on his own and returning to a home and family that, while providing sustenance and shelter, can be harsh, binding, and cold.

Central Park, then, falls between Holden's childhood home and his forays into the adult world of New York City, geographically and emotionally. He knows the area like the "back of (his) hand" from when he used to ride his bike and "roller-skate there all the time" (200). Yet the park at the end of his desperate night serves only to reinforce his loneliness, isolation, and deteriorating mental and physical health. Desperate to find the pond and the ducks, Holden nearly stumbles into the water, drops and breaks Phoebe's special record (an event he characterizes as "something terrible"), and begins to fear he might catch pneumonia and die from exposure. "It was just very cold and nobody around anywhere," he tells the reader as he begins his short walk to his parent's apartment building. Although Holden is compelled to sneak into the apartment in order to avoid his parents, it is very clear that he immediately finds refuge from the cold and inhospitable night. "I certainly knew I was home.... Our foyer has a funny smell that doesn't smell like anyplace else. I don't know what the hell it is. It isn't cauliflower and it isn't perfume—I don't know what the hell it is—but you always know you are home" (205). These intimate sensory details contrast strongly with the unwelcome city ("vomity" smelling cabs, for instance) and his memories of Pencey (especially Ackley's ripe socks) and potently recall Holden's history of being exiled from his boyhood home and the memories that register so strongly on our senses. The theme of flight and homelessness—and the search for a refuge—continues when Phoebe figures out that Holden has once again been kicked out of school. "Daddy's gonna kill you" she cries repeatedly. Holden tries to reassure Phoebe, and himself, that he is in control:

> "I'll be away," he tells her. "I'll be—I'll probably be in Colorado on this ranch."
> "Don't make me laugh," she says. "You can't even ride a horse."
> "Who can't? Sure I can. Certainly I can. They can teach you in about two minutes." (216)

Holden is more confident in his ability to ride a powerful animal he has probably never even touched than to negotiate the rough and tumble trails toward adulthood. Earlier in the novel Holden had the same trouble "explaining" to his girl friend Sally Hayes his disdain for authority, trends, and social expectations, asking her if she ever got "fed up" with the city, all the material things, and all the phonies. "You know something," he tells her. "You're probably the only reason I'm in New York right now, or anywhere. If you weren't around, I'd probably be someplace way the hell off. In the woods or some goddam place" (170). Sally doesn't share

Holden's vision, however, and she cannot even fathom the prospect of starting out alone and without purpose, plans, or even a place to live. "You can't just do something like that," she says. "In the first place, we're both practically children. We'll have oodles of time to do those things—all those things. I mean, after you go to college and all" (173). Sally does not recognize how desperate Holden is for a place where he can grip the reins, rather than be reined in, and where he can build some *place* "way the hell off" constructed on his own terms, not the expectations of a society he thinks is phony and hollow. His unrealistic impulse to escape to the woods or the West echoes Horwitz's argument that mother nature will "take care" of you in a way that humans cannot. In the back of Holden's mind, however, must be the ever-present and crushing memory of how mother nature has "taken care" of his brother Allie.

Like Holden, John Grady Cole in *All The Pretty Horses* is driven by a loss of control in his life and home, also as the result of a loved one's death. The novel opens with elaborate detail of the burial of John Grady's grandfather—the man who has basically served as his father for the past several years—on a blustery, inhospitable day in southeast Texas. A similar amount of detail is provided in the opening pages to chart the long family legacy of the ranch in San Angelo, about to end with his mother's sale of the unprofitable ranch. In John Grady's case, not only is he dispossessed of the only home he has ever known right on the heels of his beloved grandfather's death, his future role on the ranch and his link to the past are shattered as well. He begs his mother to lease the ranch to him, but she replies much like Sally does to Holden:

> You're sixteen years old, you can't run a ranch.
> Yes I can.
> You're being ridiculous. You have to go to school. (15)

A similar conversation is repeated when he visits the family lawyer, Mr. Franklin. There's nothing he can do for the boy, he tells him, emphasizing to John Grady that "you're a minor," and besides, he advises him, "not everybody thinks that life on a cattle ranch in west Texas is the second best thing to dyin and goin to heaven" (17). It is through the lawyer that he learns his parents have been formally divorced, and it quickly becomes clear to the reader that John Grady, much like Holden Caulfield, finds himself homeless, longing to control his world on his own terms. His father has drifted in and out of his life and now faces an unnamed terminal illness, and his mother is most interested in pursuing her acting career and, as Mr. Franklin puts it, "she's a young woman and my guess is that she'd like to have a little more social life than what she's had to get used to" (17). Like Holden, John Grady is forced to either accept the will of others, despite his protests of independence and advanced maturity, to "sell out" by accepting the formal paths of school, marriage and social life—or risk losing what little family and home life he has left.[3]

The "old west" that Holden fantasizes about with Sally and Phoebe, however, is a *real* option to John Grady: he can escape to the "past" of old Mexico, where horses still rule the roads in a land he imagines is free of the modern taint of post-war materialism. San Angelo, to John Grady, has become an industrialized war zone with the open range replaced by roads and barbed wire fences and oil prospectors tearing it up with their trucks, derricks, and pumpjacks. Holden's sense that horses are somehow "human" allies him with John Grady, who sees the exchange of the mechanical for the animal as the first step in the separation of humans from nature. Horses are the breathing, soulful antithesis to the noisy and polluting automobiles that are partly responsible for John Grady's failed love life even as they facilitate Stradlater's. When John Grady and Rawlins first hit the trail, they cross obstacle after obstacle related to the increasing car culture and closing of the range: fencelines have to be pulled, busy highways have to be crossed, discarded motor parts have to be stepped over. "How the hell do they expect a man to ride a horse in this country?" Rawlins asks. "They don't" is John Grady's reply. Further down the trail, Rawlins wonders what the folks are doing back "home," and John Grady muses "Probably struck oil. I'd say they're in town about now pickin out their new cars and all" (37). Much later in the novel John Grady asserts to the Mexican captain that he has no driver's license. "I never did have one," he says with some contempt (169).

Although clearly out of their element crossing the highway-scarred landscape, as John Grady and Rawlins near the Rio Grande and Mexico, they blend into the landscape, in control of their destinies through the very animals beneath them. The symbolic sense of "reining" in nature has not been lost on critics who contrast John Grady's mastery over horses to his lack of control over social circumstances, his love life, and family relationships. Unsure of his footing in modern adult society, John Grady not only chooses his direction on horseback, he symbolically brings nature to his will in his near-mythic ability to "break" horses.[4] Its little wonder, then, that John Grady and Rawlins take their escape with high confidence and with little certain direction—their map of the southwest region, after all, is uncharted below Texas, open and ready to be filled in by their experiences. Unlike Holden's desperate and lonely escape, their adventure begins with a sense of excitement, promise, and camaraderie. In contrast to Holden's lone outcry to his "moron" schoolmates, their poetic flight begins with immense beauty and thrilling potential:

> They rode out along the fenceline and across the open pastureland. The leather creaked in the morning cold. They pushed the horses into a lope. The lights fell away behind them. They rode out on the high prairie where they slowed the horses to a walk and the stars swarmed around them out of the blackness. They heard somewhere in the tenantless night a bell that tolled and ceased where no bell was and they rode out on the round dais of the earth which alone was dark and no light to it and which carried their figures and bore them up into the swarming stars so that they rode not under but among them and they rode at once jaunty and circumspect, like thieves newly loosed in that dark electric, like young thieves in a glowing orchard, loosely jacketed against the cold and ten thousand worlds for the choosing. (30)

The excitement of striking out on their own fills the early passages of the book, but Rawlins and John Grady soon discover, just as Holden does, that controlling the direction one travels is not the same as controlling the direction of one's life. The rules and conventions of a society that has disappointed them and abandoned them are as inescapable as their own inevitable slide towards adulthood. For this reason, the theme of controlling time, either standing still (captured in a museum diorama, for example) or moving backwards (a rolling colonial hacienda in rural Mexico, lost in 19th-century customs and cultures) plays a major role in these novels.

For example, despite Holden's constant attempts to "pass" as older than sixteen (usually unsuccessfully, despite his graying hair and tall stature), a major portion of his solitary weekend shows an obsession with preserving time and innocence. Nothing captures this sentiment more than Holden's aching nostalgia toward the Museum of Natural History, where the displays never changed—the Eskimo and the Indian, the bird and the deer—always frozen in the same comforting pose. "Nobody'd be different," Holden recalls. "The only thing that would be different would be you" (158). Near the end of the novel Holden rushes into to the museum and immediately heads for the mummy exhibit—yet another symbol of the preservation of the body against time and change—only to confront social corruption (more graffiti), false expectations (the children he meets are afraid of the exhibits), and physical illness (he gets sick in the bathroom and passes out). This pattern is repeated later when Holden visits Phoebe's school—his old school—where he remarks that "it was exactly the same as it was when I went there" (259). The childlike innocence of his memory is undercut, once again, by still more graffiti scratched into the school walls. Try as he might, Holden cannot erase the marks that signify— to him at least—a futile battle against the encroaching concerns—and corruptions—of the adult world. "Certain things should stay the way they are," he argues. "You ought to be able to stick them in one of those big glass cases and just leave them alone" (158). The final image Holden leaves of his lost weekend is watching his sister reach for the "golden ring" while "Oh, Marie!" plays in the background. "It played that same song about fifty years ago when I was a little kid," explains Holden. "That's one nice thing about carrousels, they always play the same songs" (272). The image of Holden seemingly at peace, prepared to return home, comfortable in a familiar and childlike setting is undercut by Holden's impression that his own childhood feels "fifty years" away. The many losses and traumas in his sixteen years have not only robbed him of being a "kid," they have cast time and the future as an enemy and heightened his anxiety over future despair, crowding out the possibility of a brighter tomorrow.

In *All the Pretty Horses*, the overriding presence of time—marching forward without control, standing still, even turning backwards—is a stressed throughout the novel by McCarthy's attention to clocks and timepieces in many key scenes. The opening scene finds John Grady viewing the body of his dead grandfather, candlelit, with images of the family forebears along the wall, and a very real sense of time lost and changing: "Inside the house there was no sound save the ticking of the mantel clock in the front room" (3). A few pages later, John Grady sits in his grandfather's study, absorbed in the night-sounds of the rural San Angelo, contemplating the inevitable decision of his mother to sell the ranch, all the while fidgeting with a small brass calendar stuck on September 13th—presumably the day of his grandfather's death—and the clock striking an hour before midnight at the end of the hall (the first of many instances when this unique hour is stressed). A few days later, after dinner dishes are cleared, John Grady pleads with his mother to let him try and save the ranch and run it himself; the scene is signaled, again, by a ticking clock (15).

Trying to gain some insight into his mother's perspective before the ranch is sold, John Grady hitch-hikes to San Antonio to see her perform in a stage play. He asks a waitress: "Is it the same time here as it is in San Angelo?" The waitress cannot answer, but a man at the counter answers repeatedly: "It's the same time…. Same time…. Same time" (20). This obscure train of conversation reinforces John Grady's sense that time is working against him and that any attempts to control the course of his future must be considered on a broader plain, geographically and spiritually. The man sitting at the counter signals that moving laterally won't bring the necessary change of time and place; in fact, each time zone heading east *adds* an hour. To head "west," John Grady must ironically now descend south, to a wholly different place and time all together (McCarthy's interest in crossing such borders of geographic time and place is reflected in the title of his first western, *Blood Meridian*). Therefore, it is not surprising that once John Grady and Rawlins hit the trail in March, careful details about clocks, watches, and time are replaced by imagery of nature's eternal mechanism, calculated by the position of celestial landmarks. The tense night when the three young men are preparing to steal back Blevins's horse, for instance, prompts such star-gazing concern about the present and the future as the moon descends and they sit huddled in the dark, smoking. John Grady watches the stars as Rawlins asks him what time it is. "First quarter moon sets at midnight where I come from," replies John Grady.

Throughout the novel there has been attention paid to the hour before midnight, the contemplative moments before major life events and yet one more step toward the hard lessons of adulthood. While Rawlins and Blevins rest up for the planned sunrise heist, John Grady cannot sleep and instead studies the skies for more insight about passing time and life.

> He sat watching the firmament unscroll up from behind the blackened palisades of the mountains to the east. Toward the village all was darkness. Not even a dog barked. He looked at Rawlins rolled asleep in his soogan and he knew that he was right in all he'd said and there was no help for it and the dipper standing at the northern edge of the world turned and the night was a long time passing. (81)

Once Blevins splits from the boys on his recaptured mount, they travel further and further south, time rolling back as they retreat from the conveniences of the modern world into an isolated preserve of Mexico's colonial past. After travelling south over 200 miles, weathering storms and gunfire, John Grady and Rawlins stumble upon a living diorama of sorts: The Hacienda de Nuestra Señora de la Purisima Concepción—eleven thousand hectares that have been in Don Héctor Rocha's family for 170 years. The hacienda immediately fits the bill of what the family lawyer had remarked earlier in the novel: the idea of a cattle ranch as second only to "dyin and going to heaven." After being welcomed by the vaqueros working the place, grabbing grub in the ancient mess hall, settling in to their assigned bunks on the first night they arrive, Rawlins asks "How long do you think you'd like to stay here?" and John Grady responds: "About a hundred years" (96).

For a brief and beautiful period John Grady staves off the intrusions of 20th-century life; his skill and knowledge about horses and ranching are appreciated, relevant, and impressive in a way he had never found in Texas. In this section of the novel, McCarthy portrays the landscape and the day-to-day life on the ranch, the invigorating and close work with the horses, and John Grady's developing love affair with the hacendado's daughter in breathtaking and lyrical terms; time and care are literally lost in the good fortune of the two boys. The first time John Grady is invited into the ranch house to visit with Don Hector, however, the clock imagery returns: "The house was cool and quiet and smelled of wax flowers. A tallcase clock stood in the hallway to the left. The brass weights stirred behind the casement doors, the pendulum slowly swept" (112). After his conversation with the hacendado, he is separated from Rawlins to Don Hector's private stables, closer to civilization once again, and—despite the luck of his promotion—this is where his troubles begin, when his pursuit of Don Hector's teenage daughter begins in earnest. When she convinces him to let her ride the prized stallion he has been put in charge of, he tells her, "your fixin to get me in trouble," to which she replies, "you are in trouble" (131). Indeed, the paradise that John Grady has found—a refuge from modern time and personal loss—is being risked by his attention to Alejandra and her legacy, clearly off-limits to a ranch-hand, let alone a poor, teenage white boy from post-World War II Texas.

When John Grady is invited for a chess game in the ranch house with the Dueña Alfonsa—the grandaunt and godmother to Alejandra, and her protector—it soon becomes clear that her mission is to remind John Grady of his place in the unique world—and time—of the hacienda; her very presence "invested it with oldworld ties and with antiquity and tradition" (132). After several hours of chess and polite conversation, the Dueña exposes a silver wristwatch to check the late hour and begins speaking of her own past, and the traditions of her culture, and the unique status of the hacienda as a place out of time, a world unto itself: "Whatever my appearance may suggest, I am not a particularly oldfashioned woman. Here we live in a small world. A close world. Alejandra and I disagree strongly. Quite strongly in fact. She is much like me at that age and I seem at times to be struggling with my own past self" (135). Then she lowers the boom on John Grady about the inappropriateness of being seen with Alejandra: "She leaned back. He could hear the clock ticking in the hall. There was no sound from the kitchen. She sat watching him." He asks, "what do you want me to do?" She answers, "I want you to be considerate of a young girl's reputation," making it clear that the girl is off limits. John Grady boldly argues his case, saying it is "not right" for Alejandra to have no choice in the matter, forgetting the time warp he has entered, where all the pleasures of the hacienda are countered by the rigid social order of 19th-century colonialism. "It is not a matter of right" Dueña Alfonsa explains. "You must understand. It is a matter of who must say. In this matter I get to say. I am the one who gets to say." All during her speech, the reader is drawn to the sound of a clock ticking in the hallway, signaling the battle for control over John Grady's future, his past, and his present (136–37).

The Dueña's lesson must have had an impact on John Grady, for when Alejandra sneaks into his stable quarters five nights later, the first thing he asks her is: "What time is it?" Alejandra, eager to escape the outdated social constraints placed upon her replies, "I don't know. Eleven or something." (139) If Alejandra does not care "what hour" or "what time" it is, John Grady—like Holden—finds himself powerless and facing, once again, the hour before that figurative "midnight," when all will once again be lost to him. With little concern for the "time" she is living in, she returns "every night for nine nights running, pushing the door shut and latching it and turning the slatted light at God knew what hour and stepping out of her clothes and sliding cool and naked against him in the narrow bunk all softness and perfume and the lushness of her black hair falling over him and no caution to her at all" (142). Soon after he begins his affair with Alejandra, he and Rawlins are dragged away by armed guards, and what appears to be a genuine opportunity to cheat time and earn control over his life and home is all lost. By the end of the novel John Grady will have faced

his own death, participated in the death of another, and have been denied
Alejandra—an unwelcome and, once again, homeless, outsider. As he
recalls his sorrowful tale to the young Mexican children he shares his lunch
with after leaving the hacienda for the final time: "Donde vive? said the
oldest boy. He mused on the question. They waited. I once lived at a great
hacienda, he told them, but now I have no place to live" (243). Not only
has he lost his home, John Grady has sacrificed a significant part of his
youth in his travels. When he returns to Texas, alone, his "lost time" is
dramatically illustrated when he has to ask some townspeople not for the
hour, but for the date. Learning that it is Thanksgiving Day, readers are
astonished to know that all the action, events, and tragedies in this young
man's life occurred in the space of a scant seven months.

As both John Grady and Holden's adventures end, we are left with a
sense of loss—of home and innocence—and of time that has escaped
control. *The Catcher in the Rye* ends with Holden returning to his elementary
school, the museum, the carrousel—unable to connect to his past or find
comfort or control in his future. Mentally and physically taxed, he listens to
his kid sister. "Did you mean it what you said? You really aren't going away
anywhere? Are you really going home afterwards?" Holden confesses that
he "meant it, too. I wasn't lying to her. I really did go home afterwards"
(274). John Grady, in contrast, has no home to return to. When he reaches
San Angelo, he laments that his experiences have stripped away his youth
and exiled him from the landscape that built his childhood: "This is still
good country," Rawlins tells him. "Yeah. I know it is. But it aint my
country," John Grady answers. "Where is your country?" asks Rawlins. "I
dont know," says John Grady. "I dont know where it is. I dont know what
happens to country" (299).

Innocence and Youth

> He stood at the window of the empty cafe
> and watched the activities of the square and
> said that it was good that God kept the truths
> of life from the young as they were starting
> out or else they'd have no heart to start at all.
>
> — John Grady Cole

> All the kids kept trying to grab for the gold
> ring, and so was Phoebe, and I was sort of
> afraid she'd fall off the goddam horse, but I
> didn't say anything or do anything. The thing
> with kids is, if they want to grab for the gold
> ring, you have to let them do it, and not say
> anything.
>
> — Holden Caulfield

Each of the two epigraphs above points to the end of its respective novel and the primary concern of both Salinger and McCarthy with the themes of innocence and youth. John Grady Cole looks out a window in a small cafe in Los Picos, the last Mexican village before his return to Texas. He's watching a wedding party take place in the rain, and he sees the children playing—sees the hopeful expressions of the teenage bride and groom as they pose to preserve their happy moment to film—and is saddened by thoughts of lost youth. "In the sepia monochrome of a rainy day in that lost village they'd grown old instantly" (284). Holden similarly seems to have accepted the final inevitability of growing up in watching the children reach for the "gold ring." These quotes reveal the compelling desire of both Holden and John Grady to protect and preserve youth, and their obsessive anxiety over the fate of children and the adulthood that awaits them. If John Grady and Holden have been cheated out of a fulfilling childhood, they seem intent on insuring that others are not subjected to the same.

While the heroes of these novels want to shelter their young charges from the corruption of the adult world, the actions, thoughts, and seemingly innocent insights of even younger "protectees" provide some of the most dramatic, moving—and mature—lessons in each novel. Jimmy Blevins in *All the Pretty Horses* and Phoebe in *The Catcher in the Rye* (and in poignant memories, Holden's dead brother Allie) share abilities, skills, intellect, and mature insight that make them seem much older than they actually are, yet many of their actions often betray their youth and innocence. When John Grady and Rawlins finally confront their interloper on the trail, they are surprised to find thirteen-year-old Jimmy Blevins, noticeably out of place on a prized bay horse, an expensive and mature mount that the child handles like an adult. "He aint as green as he looks," Rawlins remarks to John Grady (43). They are even more surprised when he draws an elaborate 32–20 Colt Bisley with gutta-percha grips and his small hand fires a bullet through Rawlins's billfold tossed in the air (47). Yet Blevins reveals his childish side as well—falling off of a bench at the dinner table, his horse when he is drunk—and although he may seem unafraid of an angry Mexican posse, he has an irrational fear of lightning, which triggers the loss of his horse, and most of his clothes, and which threatens the safety of the entire group as they plan to sneak into the Mexican village of Encantada to steal back his belongings. "I'll say one thing about him," Rawlins remarks, with about as much compliment as he can muster. "That little son of a bitch wouldnt stand still for nobody high-jackin his horse" (88).

While not as brazen or colorful as Jimmy Blevins, Phoebe in *The Catcher in the Rye*, is one of a long line of Salinger wunderkinder whose age is belied by their actions and insight. She can dance like an adult, prefers "grown up" movies like *The 39 Steps*, fancies herself a writer, has an elaborate and active imagination, and it is her therapy and insight that Holden seeks at the end of his disastrous night in Manhattan, when he's feeling cold, alone, and obsessed with death. She cheers him up but throws a tantrum upon hearing he has been kicked out of school again; she chides him for his language, his inability to stay out of trouble, and forces him to confront his antisocial attitude: "You don't like *anything* that's happening" (220). Holden argues his case but is stymied by images of James Castle jumping to his death or the prospects of becoming a "phony" lawyer or scientist. Finally, it is Phoebe who gets Holden to open up and declare the one thing he would "like to be" even while correcting his reading of the Robert Burns poem (224).

The prominent use of these characters who behave as children one instance and adults the next is in keeping with the emphasis both McCarthy and Salinger place on the themes of lost youth and innocence and the roles of both Holden and John Grady as "protectors" of children who are poised to lose both. Holden, for instance, tries repeatedly to erase the profanity on the school and museum walls. The thought of this corruption in the literal "halls" of childhood affects Holden so severely that he nearly loses his mind in murderous rage which, like his attempt to smash a toothbrush through Stradlater's throat, reaches a depth of surprising violence:

> It drove me damn near crazy. I thought how Phoebe and all the other little kids would see it, and how they'd wonder what the hell it meant, and then finally some dirty kid would tell them—all cockeyed, naturally—what it meant, and how they'd all think about it and maybe even worry about it for a couple of days. I kept wanting to kill whoever'd written it. I figured it was some perverty bum that'd sneaked into the school late at night to take a leak or something and then wrote it on the wall. I kept picturing myself catching him at it, and how I'd smash his head on the stone steps till he was good and goddam dead and bloody. (262–61)

Holden is more than just upset in these passages; these threats to innocence are connected to images of throats torn open, heads bashed to pulp—deadly and gruesome physical violence. When Holden encounters the profanity once again scrawled on the museum wall, a place nearly sacred to him in its preservation of time and innocence, we sense an exasperation, defeat and angst that sink to the depths of his depression, marking him beyond death. "I think, even, if I ever die, and they stick me in a cemetery, and I have a tombstone and all, it'll say 'Holden Caulfield' on it and then what year I was born and what year I died, and then right under that it'll say 'Fuck You.' I'm positive in fact" (204).

Similar signs of corruption and threats to innocence occur throughout *All the Pretty Horses*. John Grady spends much of the first portion of the novel trying to stick up for Blevins and protect him from Rawlins's constant ribbing and scorn; most of their troubles, risks, and sacrifices find their source in John Grady's unwillingness to abandon the young boy. After surviving the thunderstorm, for instance, there is a sign that clearly indicates the three riders are treading towards trouble:

> Bye and bye they passed a stand of roadside cholla against which small birds had been driven by the storm and there impaled. Gray nameless birds espaliered in attitudes of stillborn flight or hanging loosely in their feathers. Some of them were still alive and they twisted on their spines as the horses passed and raised their heads and cried out but the horsemen rode on. (73)

The next scene answers this omen by introducing a rough-looking group of Mexican laborers gathering desert plants to boil and refine into wax. While the workers share their beans and tortillas, they eye Blevins, who is sitting aside, sunburned, in his underwear. John Grady is asked by one of the workers if the boy is a relative or a friend, and then he is made an indecent offer. He immediately gathers Blevins and Rawlins to make a cordial, but hasty, exit: "No one spoke. When they were clear of the camp a mile or so Blevins asked what it was that the man in the vest had wanted but John Grady didn't answer." When Blevins persists, Rawlins answers, "He wanted to buy you. That's what he wanted." An uncomfortable silence follows: "John Grady didn't look at Blevins. They rode on in silence. What did you go and tell him that for? said John Grady. There wasnt no call to do that" (77). With shades of Holden, John Grady feels an overwhelming responsibility to not only protect Blevins from physical harm but to sustain his "innocent" outlook on life by shielding him from the corruptions and perversities of adult life. These fathering impulses continue once they are all thrown in jail together. While Rawlins turns against Blevins, John Grady remains cool and continues to give Blevins the benefit of the doubt, shields him from Rawlin's wrath, and tries to convince him that he won't "hang" like Rawlins suggests. When John Grady meets the captain, he is asked a series of questions about Blevins's age and relationship which echoes the conversation at the waxcamp. When the captain notes that Blevins "don't have no feathers," John Grady is slow, at first, to understand this reference to Blevin's sexual immaturity and angers the captain when he indignantly replies: "I wouldn't know about that. It dont interest me" (167).

The Catcher in the Rye similarly focuses attention on such moments when youngsters confront perverse or sexual situations which are ambiguous or uncertain. When Holden wakes up to find his former teacher, Mr. Antolini, caressing his hair, he can't be certain—he later admits—if he was really making a "flitty pass" at him or not. Salinger paints the situation vague and ambiguous, capturing the sense of the child facing the actions and motives of the adult world with such uncertainty. One gesture could be perfectly innocent while the next could be corrupt—and Holden, like many boys his age, knows "more damn perverts, at schools and all, than anybody you ever met, and their always being perverty when *I'm* around" (249). These are the threats that Holden and John Grady seem so obsessed with trying to shelter the children from. Their failures to prevent such perversity or protect the innocent lead to their own moral tests. Holden's murderous rage directed towards the writer of the "fuck you" is similar to the moral test John Grady faces when he has the opportunity to kill the perverse captain, his hostage, later in the novel. Like Holden, John Grady recognizes the irony of fighting violence and perversity with more violence. "I aint going to kill you," he tells the captain. "I'm not like you" (278).

Of course, John Grady is tested in ways that Holden never is, particularly when he is forced to kill a man in Saltillo prison. "I never thought I'd do that," he confesses to Rawlins after they are freed from the prison. "You didnt have no choice," Rawlins argues. "He'd of done it to you." John Grady can't accept this reasoning: "You dont need to try and make it right. It is what it is" (215). Here the tie to murdered innocence is beautifully captured when John Grady explains that he bought the knife with "Blevins's money" that he had pulled out of his boot as he was being dragged off to his execution. Rawlins, who had been so hard on Blevins, is also traumatized by the event and confesses to John Grady that he can't get the image out of his head—the trauma is written in his seventeen-year-old face, which now looks "old and sad" to John Grady. "I cant believe they just walked him out there and done him that way," he cries. "I keep thinking about how scared he was." John Grady reassures him that he'll feel better when he gets back "home" to Texas. "Rawlins shook his head and looked out the window again. I dont think so, he said" (212). If Rawlins has aged instantly through these experiences, John Grady's own lost youth and innocence is even more explicitly tied to the death of the young boy. "I aint Blevins" he assures Rawlins, as he makes plans to return for the horses and the girl. "Yeah, said Rawlins. I know you aint. But I wonder how much better off you are than him" (213). As Rawlins intuits, the physical death of Jimmy Blevins signals the spiritual death of John Grady's last inner child. When he returns to Texas, John Grady confesses to a judge his guilt over not only killing the boy at the prison but his desire to kill the Mexican captain. "I wasnt even mad at him. Or I didnt feel like I was. That boy he shot, I didnt hardly even know him. I felt bad about it. But he wasnt nothing to me" (292). The judge asks why he would want to kill him if that were the case. Finally, John Grady confesses that he is most upset with his failed mission to protect Blevins—and by extension, that boy's innocence—and by further extension, the innocent boy in himself. "The reason I wanted to kill him was because I stood there and let him walk that boy out in the trees and shoot him and I never said nothin" (293).

John Grady's failure to protect Blevins—the very idea that he *could*, somehow, protect him—brings to mind the image of Holden, the "only big kid around" trying to keep those kids from falling off the cliff. Some critics have argued that Holden "wants" to be the catcher in the rye, or that he "desires" to play this role; it is his "fantasy" or "dream," an unrealistic vocation and distracting preoccupation. Careful attention to Salinger's language is important here, however, for the precise term that Holden uses with Phoebe is that he'd *"like"* to be the catcher in the rye, that is, if "he had (his) goddamn choice" (which reinforces his realistic and painful understanding that he has no goddamn choice). Salinger is notoriously careful in his selection of words and in his revision process, so having Holden use the word "like" is an important distinction, for it paints this famous metaphor in two distinct ways, highlighting Holden's altruism—his willingness to sacrifice himself in order to protect others from the experiences and growing pains that he has suffered—and reaffirming the underlying source of his angst, that he knows that he *can't* be the catcher in the rye. What he truly "wants" or "desires" is for the "crazy cliff" not to exist at all. Nor does he see his job as "fun" but an obligation where he "has" to be there to catch the kids. All day long, what he "has" to do is protect them from the cliff. His language illustrates that he is not deluded into believing he can preserve his own youth and innocence; these have already been destroyed. Young readers are drawn to Holden because they sympathize with him on an intuitive level—even if they do not always readily admit it—that days of careless youth are numbered, and the reality of inevitable initiation, growth, and loss of childhood is a universal condition. When readers rediscover the book years later, it may affect them even deeper, as parents who view their children sleeping in their beds at night can nearly hear the rye rustling in the breeze as they stand at the edge of that crazy cliff, wondering where the time goes and wishing that they could catch their own children as they play forth and out of their control, before their eyes, down the same path all must tread.

Nearly fifty years later, this very same sentiment is captured in *All the Pretty Horses* when John Grady, stuck in a Mexican jail cell, dreams of running through expansive and Edenic fields surrounded by cliffs; in this case the high mesas are covered with wildflowers and prairie clover instead of rye, and thundering herds of horses have replaced the galloping groups of children. In both dreams, the heady experience of running, playing, and living without restraint or fear of falling is at the center of the image:

> That night he dreamt of horses in a field on a high plain where the spring rains had brought up the grass and the wildflowers out of the ground and the flowers ran all blue and yellow far as the eye could see and in the dream he was among the horses running and in the dream he himself could run with the horses

and they coursed the young mares and fillies over the plain where their rich bay and their rich chestnut colors shone in the sun and the young colts ran with their dams and trampled down the flowers in a haze of pollen that hung in the sun like powdered gold and they ran he and the horses out along the high mesas where the ground resounded under their running hooves and they flowed and changed and ran and their manes and tails blew off of them like spume and there was nothing else at all in that high world and they moved all of them in a resonance that was like a music among them and they were none of them afraid horse nor colt nor mare and they ran in that resonance which is the world itself and which cannot be spoken but only praised. (161–62)

John Grady's dream, like Holden's, confronts the rude reality of the world, however, when he wakes up to find his best friend being led from the cell to meet his interrogators. Appropriately, this is the first and only time in the book that the narrative leaves John Grady's perspective. The reader follows Rawlins, and John Grady is left behind, helpless to protect his friend, unable to stop the process that will lead to Blevins's execution, caged in a cell rather than running free on a high mesa, facing a precipitous cliff and unable to stop, or catch his companions, should they fall.

Love and Death

> "Allie, don't let me disappear. Allie, don't let me disappear. Allie, don't let me disappear. Please, Allie."
> — Holden Caulfield

> Rawlins nodded. You think about all the stuff that can happen to you, he said. There aint no end to it.
> — *All the Pretty Horses*

The way Salinger and McCarthy represent the weighty issues of love and death—and their persistent connection—reflects a post-war consciousness (appropriate to their historical setting) influenced by modernism and its suspicions of technology over theology, science over the soul, meaninglessness over meaning, biology over romantic love. Moreover—as many critics and theorists have pointed out—both artists reveal the influence of authors such as Melville, Fitzgerald, Faulkner, and (Holden's criticisms aside) Hemingway—artists who put the very meaning of love, and death, up to question. As the above quotes illustrate, these characters share an existential quest far deeper than just hitting the trail or horsing around (pardon the pun, but as we have seen repeatedly, horses represent the physical nature of the universe—and become the very symbol attached to love and death—in McCarthy's novel).

While much of the popularity of *The Catcher in the Rye* can be traced to Holden's romantic adventures, his love life is, in fact, the locus of his most violent and dark experiences and thoughts. His claim "I'm probably the biggest sex maniac you ever saw," is illustrated when, within hours of fleeing Pencey for New York, he has tried to invite the mother of one of his classmates to the club car on the train for a drink, witnessed the sexual horseplay in the windows of his hotel, called a woman named Faith Cavendish who "wasn't exactly a whore or anything but that didn't mind doing it once in a while," (83) and flirted with three tourists from Seattle in the hotel lounge (who dance with him but don't take seriously his romantic advances). After this energetic start, however, the reader begins to see that Holden's sexual mania has less to do with appetite and libido than an obsession with lost innocence and his inability to square the physical realities of sex with his idealized conceptions of "love."

Holden acknowledges his conflicted attitude towards his own emerging sexuality with the "*very* crumby stuff" he "wouldn't mind doing if the opportunity came up" (81). The perversity of such desires confronts his inexperienced and innocent view of physical relationships: "I think if you don't really like a girl, you shouldn't horse around with her at all, and if you *do* like her, then you're supposed to like her face, and if you like her face, you ought to be careful about doing crumby stuff to it, like squirting water all over it." (32). One face he obsesses over is Jane Gallagher's. Asserting their relationship wasn't "anything *physical* or anything" (99), Holden cannot get Jane out of his mind and still relives the passion and connection in the holding of hands or the sweet gesture of her palm resting on his neck at a movie and, especially, the afternoon when he comes "close to necking" with her as she cries over some unspecified abuse by her "booze hound" father. "The next thing I knew," Holden explains, "I was kissing her all over—*any*where—her eyes, her *nose*, her forehead, her eyebrows and all, her *ears*—her whole face except her mouth and all. She sort of wouldn't let me get to her mouth" (102). As moving and emotional as the scene is, Holden's tender kisses all over this face he idolizes coupled with his awkward attempt, and her refusal, to kiss her mouth seem almost sordid. Even as Holden attempts to be the "catcher in the rye" with Jane—yet another attempt to protect an innocent from the perversity and abuse of the adult world—he can't control his own physical urges, bringing to mind the second (unmentioned) verse of the Burns poem: "if a body kiss a body, need a body cry?"[5] That Holden admits his most ideal romantic moment occurs when Jane is suffering from emotional (if not sexual) abuse cues his own psychosexual conflict.

Ultimately, Holden is confused—perhaps even wounded—by the thought of his love interests having sexual desires of their own. He's obviously wrestled with this dichotomy before, describing girls as "dumb" when they get passionate, their sexual abandon not being compatible with his idealized and innocent sense of romance. Holden also reflects the modern anxiety over the "science" of sex itself—Darwin to Freud, sexual selection to unconscious drives—suspecting that "love" has less to do with the heart than with hormones. His confession that "Sex is something I really don't understand too hot" reminds us that his mania, in the modern sense, would be traced either to his repressed desires or his inability to accept the biological reality of sexual selection, neither of which would comfort his obsession with Jane Gallagher. His conflicted attitudes are reflected in his blunt questioning of how aggressive and domineering the male should be: "You never know whether they really *want* you to stop, or whether they're just scared as hell, or whether they're just telling you to stop so that if you *do* go through with it, the blame'll be on you, not them" (120–21). Fear, blame, stop, go—hardly the vocabulary of a romantic idealist. While Holden certainly does not admire Stradlater's "professional secrets," he recognizes that physical beauty and sexual aggression are facts of nature hard to deny. Long before his jealousy and competition with Stradlater, after all, Holden had been unable to fathom how Jane could be attracted to Al Pike, who is "all muscles and no brains" (175). Holden's image of Jane sitting at children's game of checkers—innocent, vulnerable, wounded—is shattered by the possibility that she might have matured an attraction for powerful, handsome boys. No wonder Holden gets so upset when Stradlater remarks "What the hell ya think we did all night—play checkers, for Chrissake?" (55). Holden himself admits his need to emerge from this sexual pre-adolescence when he meets up with Carl Luce, an old schoolmate notorious for his late night "sex talks." In their awkward meeting at the bar, Luce keeps telling Holden to "grow up" and advises him to get "psychoanalyzed" about his sexual hangups (though if Carl Luce is the product of a mature sexual understanding, readers can only hope that Holden stays fixated on Jane and checkers).

Young readers (especially) can no doubt sympathize with Holden's confusing sexual immaturity. The imagery of Holden struggling to remove a bra and having "a helluva lot of trouble just *find*ing what he's "looking for" captures the humor and awkwardness of adolescent sexual horseplay—and the idea that he would like to "practice" on the prostitute so that he can learn to play a woman "like a violin" humorously demonstrates Holden's naivete (122). There is little to laugh about in Holden's actual encounter with "Sunny," who—given Holden's just-stated insecurities—is the *last* person he would want to work through his sexual hangups with. She's "young as hell," about Holden's age, and all business, watching the clock, in a hurry, and not "too goddam friendly." She doesn't buy that Holden is 22 for one second, and when Holden defers the question to her age, she responds "Old enough to know better," once again striking the theme of experience over age (123).[6] Sunny's green dress hanging stark in his closet becomes yet another symbol of defaced innocence: Holden imagines the salesman thinking she was a "regular girl" when she bought it, but now its purity is tainted like a "fuck you" marked on a grade school staircase, a frank description of the transaction about to take place. "I know you're supposed to feel pretty sexy when somebody gets up and pulls their dress over their head," he notes, "but I didn't. Sexy was about the *last* thing I was feeling. I felt much more depressed than sexy" (123). Many an adolescent boy has no doubt read in disbelief when Holden resists Sunny's advances; even as she tussles his hair and calls him "cute," he longs for her to get off his lap and spend some time just talking. "She was a pretty spooky kid," he says, revealing how deeply his sexual initiation is confounded by images of lost innocence and the fearful uncertainty of the "kid" transacting life in the adult world. He would have been much better off with one of the "old bags" he warned Maurice not to send him. "Even with that little bitty voice she had, she could sort of scare you a little bit. If she'd been a big old prostitute with a lot of makeup on her face and all, she wouldn't have been half as spooky" (127).

Holden's sexual exploration leads once again to violence and humiliation when Sunny's pimp, Maurice, defied by Holden, snaps his finger "very hard" on his pajamas. "I won't tell you where he snapped it, but it hurt like hell. I told him he was a goddam dirty moron" (135). As with Stradlater, Holden loses his senses, enrages Maurice, gets beaten up, then stumbles around nursing his injury and fantasizing about his violent revenge: "he'd see me with the automatic in my hand and he'd start screaming at me, in this very high-pitched, yellow-belly voice, to leave him alone. But I'd plug him anyway. Six shots right through his fat hairy belly" (136). Holden's extremely violent reaction and abuse mirrors his earlier battle with Stradlater—where he had imagined smashing his toothbrush to split open his throat and had "felt like jumping out the window" afterward (63). While romantic and sexual jealousies are a rite of passage for most teenagers, for Holden all sex becomes fraught with perversity, humiliation, or violence—sometimes all three at once—such as when he's seated at Ernie's bar next to a "Joe Yale-looking guy" who ignores the protests and pleas of his "terrific-looking girl," and fondles her under the table while narrating a story about his dormmate trying to commit suicide (112). Throughout his weekend in New York, Holden is forced to "read" the writing on the wall where "fuck you" represents not only a violent threat to innocence but an affirmation of the basic drives in all humans that can't be erased.

In *All the Pretty Horses*, John Grady's love life is similarly complex, sometimes humiliating, and also connected to violence. Early in the story on a nighttime horse ride, Rawlins tries to comfort his friend who can't compete with the older, richer boy who has stolen his gal: "I don't know what you expect. Him two years oldern than you. Got his own car and everything" (10). John Grady agrees that (reminiscent of Al Pike in Holden's story) "There aint nothin to him. Never was," but still she has chosen him instead. "She aint worth it," Rawlins says. "None of em are." John Grady contemplates the suggestion and then—like Holden who still believes in love and romance—remarks chivalrously "Yes they are." (10). This question of sexual competition and female selection comes up repeatedly. When John Grady's father—a character who has been darkly shaped by his war experiences to see the world straight—finds out that his son is now single, he asks "she quit you or did you quit her?" John Grady says he's not sure. "That means she quit you" (24). In his last meeting with Mary Catherine, she explains "A person cant help the way they feel." This admission of physical desire confounds John Grady. When she explains that her new boyfriend is not a jealous type like John Grady, he lashes out: "That's good. That's a good trait to have. Save him a lot of aggravation" (29) Because John Grady is such a quiet and reticent character, these brief revelations are the best insight to his state of mind when it comes to his heart; like Holden, he is romantically sensitive, easily wounded, and intimidated by the prospect of sexual competition and the forces of physical attraction.

Rawlins, impatient with John Grady's romantic idealism, argues for a more practical understanding of sex: "A goodlookin horse is like a goodlookin woman. They're always more trouble than what they're worth. What a man needs is just one that will get the job done" (89). Later, when John Grady makes it clear he has intentions towards Alejandra, Rawlins argues that a poor Texas cowboy can't compete: "This one of course she

probably dates guys got their own airplanes let alone cars" (118). Rawlins's
hard assessment may have been true back in Texas, where the very image of
the car was associated with false sexual prowess, materialistic corruption,
and separation from nature. He has forgotten, however, that their world
has shifted to the hacienda, where John Grady is respected for his prowess,
and he doesn't need a car to impress Alejandra—especially when he is put
in charge of the stallion and all breeding activities on the ranch. John Grady
makes a point to ride the stallion every day during the mating period to
keep it "manageable," he convinces the hacendado, but also to impress his
daughter: "because John Grady loved to ride the horse. In truth he loved
to be seen riding it. In truth he loved for her to see him riding it" (127).[7]
This juxtaposition of the mating process and the courtship of the young
lovers—literally on horseback—provides the modern undercurrent of
biology to idealized love; horses may represent a pristine and soulful beauty
to John Grady, but anyone who has witnessed their breeding can attest to
the physicality of the act itself. Even when he is employed in the very
process of sexual reproduction, John Grady tenaciously resists this idea that
the fundamental drives in nature are directed toward this one aim of
perfecting the bloodline. He foolishly believes Alejandra will run off with
him, even though the colonial environment of the hacienda (and the
objections of the Dueña Alfonsa, who speaks so elaborately of her own lost
courtship) would never support their relationship or their offspring within
a culture that traces its lineage to the very "discovery" of the region by
Europeans. At the end of the novel John Grady still clings to the purity of
his relationship with Alejandra. When the judge asks if John Grady's
troubles didn't begin by getting Alejandra "in a family way," John Grady
responds, "No sir, I was in love with her." The judge reminds John Grady,
"you could be in love with her and still knock her up." (291).

Ultimately John Grady's romantic quests mirror Holden's and reflect
the same disillusionment at the suggestion that love in its purest sense may
not even exist. The most telling example of Holden's struggles with
idealized love vs. the reality of physical attraction—and the process of
sexual competition and selection—can be found in his reference to his

favorite book, *The Great Gatsby* (183). Jay Gatsby's relentless and idealized pursuit of Daisy (and willingness to work outside the "rules" of law or social order) is strikingly similar to Holden's obssessiveness with Jane Gallagher. The fact that Gatsby, in all his romance and good intention, couldn't overcome Daisy's sexual attraction to the strong, imposing (and thuggishly immoral) Tom Buchanan is yet another reminder that the journey into adulthood reinforces the power of sexual attraction over romanticized "love."[8] This similarly marks a journey not just into "adulthood" but into the kind of dark modernist vision that Hemingway laid bare in stories like "Soldier's Home," where the returning combat veteran, Krebs, has lost his faith in both love and God. Critics have long read the influence of Hemingway, Fitzgerald, even T.S. Eliot in Salinger's work. Perhaps it is stretching to note that one of the Seattle tourists is named Krebs—or that Hemingway's shell-shocked soldier also seeks his only relief from the weight of the world by spending time with his little sister. And like the climactic scene of "Soldier's Home," where Krebs refuses to "lie" to his mother that he loves her or anybody and is then unable to pray when she asks him to kneel with her, Holden is forced to confront the possibility that love is a sham supplanted by biological urge and that other alternatives are just as vacant. After his bout with Stradlater, obsessing over his "technique" in back car seats, he wanders into Ackley's room where he enrages him with irreverent (but seemingly earnest) questions about joining a monastery (65). Similarly, after his frustrated encounter with Sunny, Holden lies sleepless in his bed where he "felt like praying or something" but, being "sort of an atheist," is unable to do so. "I couldn't pray worth a damn. Every time I got started, I kept picturing old Sunny calling me a crumb-bumb" (130–31).

In fact Holden is affected, just as Salinger, by the heavy weight of modernism. Some critics have called it an existentialist, even nihilistic, vision; at the very least, Holden is reminded time and time again that his romantic idealism is out of place. Near the end of the novel—confused over his sexual and romantic failures and the "flitty pass" that Mr. Antolini made (or didn't make?)—Holden picks up a magazine at the train station

and starts reading an article about hormones, which he says made him feel
even more depressed. "It described how you should look, your face and
eyes and all, if your hormones were in good shape, and I didn't look that
way at all. I looked exactly like the guy in the article with lousy hormones"
(254). There has been little in Holden's weekend to persuade him that
romantic love is the foundation of adult relationships, and if "love" is
actually more about sexual selection, he wonders if he has the traits to
compete with the Stradlaters, Al Pikes, Carl Luces, and Tom Buchanans in
the world. Part of the modern dilemma facing these characters, and the
artists who crafted them, is squaring the contemporary notions of biology,
sexual selection, and psychological drives with the romantic idealism of
love.

After being freed from prison, through the arrangements and expenses
of the Dueña Alfonsa, John Grady returns to the hacienda one last time
where he thinks he is "owed an explanation" (228). In the long, elaborate
conversation he has with the Dueña, he learns about love, disfigurement,
revolution, class, betrayal, the suppression of women, society, the history of
Mexico, fate, and chance. More than anything, their conversation focuses
upon growing up and the choices—or lack of choices—that young people
face. When the Dueña was sixteen—John Grady's age when he began his
journey—she was a "freethinker" and idealist. She witnessed the poverty of
Mexico first hand and even envied the ability of the children to adapt and
still find hope for another day. "Their intelligence was frightening," she
says. "And they had a freedom which we envied. There were so few
restraints upon them. So few expectations. Then at the age of eleven or
twelve they would cease being children. They lost their childhood overnight
and they had no youth. They became very serious. As if some terrible truth
had been visited upon them. Some terrible vision" (232). Then, she
explains, "in the summer of my seventeenth year my life changed forever"
(233). Between the disfigurement of her hand in a shooting accident, and
the love won of a revolutionary, then lost—and a revolution lost—Alfonsa
shares the process that, like John Grady nearing his own seventeenth year,
resulted in her "growing up" and facing the world on its own terms. "In the

end we all come to be cured of our sentiments," she advises John Grady. "Those whom life does not cure death will. The world is quite ruthless in selecting between the dream and the reality, even where we will not. Between the wish and the thing the world lies waiting" (238).

Alfonsa's remarks—elaborate, poetic, and epic in tone—make up one of the most remarkable passages in *All the Pretty Horses,* and the stylized and metaphoric language stands in stark contrast to both the reticent speech of John Grady and Rawlins and the effusive, first-person storytelling of Holden Caulfield. But her words speak to the heart of both novels: John Grady Cole and Holden Caulfield both suffer the "cure" to their sentiments, a more realistic and mature understanding of the complex forces behind sex and love. Her stoic explanation that everyone grows up to accept the "truth" or the "reality" of the "world (that) lies waiting" and abandons the "dream" or the "wish" of childhood seems reasonable, but the painful "cure" based around experiences of death seems a treatment that nobody this young should have to endure. Though these are stories written about young people, seen through the eyes of young characters, one cannot forget how intensely important the role of death is to the trauma of Holden (it has essentially robbed him of his childhood) and John Grady (whose adult dream of running the family ranch is destroyed by the death of his grandfather). Near the end of Book I in *All the Pretty Horses,* John Grady and Rawlins, having weathered their fair share of storms and violence, turn their conversations to death:

> You ever think about dyin? [asks Rawlins]
>
> Yeah. Some. You?
>
> Yeah. Some. You think there's a heaven?
>
> Yeah. Don't you?
>
> I don't know. Yeah. Maybe. You think you can believe in heaven if you dont believe in hell?
>
> I guess you can believe what you want to.
>
> Rawlins nodded. You think about all the stuff that can happen to you, he said. There aint no end to it. (91)

There certainly seems to be "no end" to the loss in John Grady's life. *All the Pretty Horses* begins with the grandfather's funeral, features the horrific execution of thirteen-year-old Jimmy Blevins, the near-death of both John Grady and Rawlins at Saltillo prison, the death of the Mexican in the prison messhall by John Grady's hand, the death of John Grady's father as he nears the border of Texas, and the final funeral of the Abuela at the end of the book—not to mention his expulsion from "heaven on earth," and (he believes) his destined and true love. These accumulative losses find their symbolic zenith when John Grady, nearing Texas, stops to shoot a young doe to nourish his battered, trail-weary body. "When he reached her she lay in her blood in the grass and he knelt with the rifle and put his hand on her neck and she looked at him and her eyes were warm and wet and there was no fear in them and then she died" (282). As he kneels by the fallen animal, John Grady gives pause to remember the events of his journey—good (life on the hacienda) and bad (life in jail), love (Alejandra) and death (Blevins, perhaps the Mexican captain). Beneath it all the landscape lies eternal:

> Grass and blood. Blood and stone. Stone and the dark medallions that the first flat drops of rain caused upon them. He remembered Alejandra and the sadness he'd first seen in the slope of her shoulders which he'd presumed to understand and of which he knew nothing and felt a loneliness he'd not known since he was a child and he felt wholly alien to the world although he loved it still. He thought that in the beauty of the world were hid a secret. He thought the world's heart beat at some terrible cost and that the world's pain and its beauty moved in a relationship of diverging equity and that in this headlong deficit the blood of multitudes might ultimately be exacted for the vision of a single flower. (282)

At this point in his journey, experience has supplanted innocence, and John Grady can assess the cost of his survival. He once had "presumed to understand" the way of the world, and now he sees, like Holden, the writing on the wall: love and beauty, violence and death, purity and prayer, blood and grass. When Holden describes visiting his brother's grave, with the cold rain percolating through the soil to his lonely body, it echoes the "terrible cost" that John Grady feels as he looks into the eyes of the young doe: "It was awful. It rained on his lousy tombstone, and it rained on the grass on his stomach." Death indeed cures Holden of all sentiment, uncomforted by the hope that "it is only his body and all that's in the cemetery, and his soul's in Heaven and all that crap" (202) His own vulgar assessment of Heaven's potential and his earlier admissions of being "sort of an atheist" make for a gut-wrenching scene, particularly when the cemetery visitors escape the rain by piling into their cars and, in the face of death, run off to catch lunch. As central as the idea of running away has been to Holden's story, imagine the anguish he feels in leaving his dead brother behind, *forever*. All the theology in the world can't overcome Holden's justified fear of disappearing.[9] Of course grass and graves have a tradition in American literature, but Holden, a young man of the twentieth century, can't quite accept the hopeful life cycle represented in the transcendent ending of "Song of Myself." Where Whitman calls his readers to look for him beneath their boot-soles, his resurrection embodied in the grass itself, Holden leaves us with cold rain soaking his brother's corpse while the living run away. Nearing the end of the twentieth century, McCarthy shares the same existential vision, grass soaked with blood, the hard-learned lesson that "those whom life does not cure, death will."

Conclusion

If both *The Catcher in the Rye* and *All the Pretty Horses* capture powerfully the forces of love and death in adolescent lives—and the stirring impulses to run away from troubles, to take control in a world that seems out of control—and the conflicting emotions of growing up while growing out of innocent childhood, what might be concluded about the way a contemporary author like McCarthy treats these subjects as opposed to the approach of Salinger in the early 1950s? In *Love and Death in the American Novel*, Leslie Fiedler noted that novelists in 1950 still focused on the fairly innocent and exciting shenanigans of teenage rebellion: sneaking out, making out, running away, pilfering, "hooking" supplies, and ditching school. "It is easy to exaggerate the difference that a few generations and the 'sexual revolution' have made in the Good Bad Boy in literature," he writes. "Even though he is allowed now a certain amount of good clean sex (not as the basis of an adult relationship but as an exhibition of prowess) and forbidden in exchange an equivalent amount of good clean violence, his standard repertory of permitted indiscretions remains pretty much the same" (289). In the fifty years since Salinger, as McCarthy's writing illustrates, the "repertory" now offers much more graphic and detailed sex and violence, not just in modern fiction but in contemporary culture as well.

However, *The Catcher in the Rye* is still one of the most frequently-banned works in high school curriculums (along with, ironically, *Huck Finn*) mostly for its often misunderstood uses of profanity. Apparently, Holden's effusive, colloquial narrative and his open questioning of adult authority and general non-conformist attitude still make the book seem dangerous to many a nervous parent or school administrator. *All the Pretty Horses*, by contrast, gets little criticism over language issues, perhaps because the writing seems more "literary," somehow less threatening since the narrative is observational and third person, told in McCarthy's majestic and challenging literary prose, and the voices of the characters themselves are reticent rather than "chatty," and profanity is rare. In fact, one of John Grady's favorite curse words is "sum buck." Trying to capture 1940s life, McCarthy chooses to make such language of his main characters unknowingly innocent, to remind us of their age (just as they feed their horses from Quaker Oats tins and mix Kool-Aid from the Rio Grande). If Holden's abrasive language distinguished him as an "authentic" voice of teendom when it was written in the 1950s, McCarthy's choice of quaint phrases and timid uses of swearing set his portrait, penned in the 1990s, as from a more "innocent period" (in comparison to the background noise of our modern cable-TV sensibilities). This, in turn, compounds the shock when such nasty things happen to these relatively hapless and harmless young men.

Where Salinger relies on language to get attention, it seems that McCarthy in the 1990s gravitates to the new social standard of disturbance: violence. Perhaps the "good clean violence" that Fiedler finds absent in the works at mid-century has now reared its ugly head; this, ultimately, is the single biggest change since Salinger. The violence in Holden's life is certainly real and painful but remembered and affected mostly by its humiliating circumstances (note how Holden parlays these moments into the romantic notion of being "shot" and suffering a cinematic fatal wound). The violence featured in McCarthy is, by contrast, more menacing and dark—the birds impaled on the cholla bush, the "matter of fact" dispatching of Jimmy Blevins with the simple "pop" of a point-blank fatal shot off in the distance. The raw violence in the Mexican prison, including John Grady's deadly knife fight, reminds us that McCarthy is writing not just about a place far removed from the world of Holden's "prep school despair," he's also writing in the decade that would culminate in the Columbine Massacre (and any number of other schoolyard shootings), a variety of mass murders and very public spectacles of violence, and the Oklahoma City bombing.

While the telling of these teen stories has changed in tone and emphasis, the importance of the storytelling itself has not. Both books burst with the sense of the need to explain, to share the loss, disillusion and disappointments—as well as the invigorating thrills of experiences acutely sensed and the lessons newly learned—that comprise the universal experience of growing up. Everyone has a story to tell; Holden begins his by asking if the reader really "wants to hear about it" at all. Readers who choose to listen learn and live a great deal through Holden's experiences, but he winds up by advising not to "tell anybody anything" as if the "nostalgia" of the memories, as Fiedler puts it, can't overcome the "terror" of the thing lost. The therapeutic effects of the talking cure seem undermined by the pain it invokes when you "start missing everybody," as Holden does (277). In *All the Pretty Horses,* John Grady and Rawlins begin with an escape into the "tenantless night" with "ten thousand worlds for the choosing" (30). Yet John Grady returns to Texas alone, a broken young man, barely alive, disabused of his romantic notions and impulses. As he nears the American border his trail no longer cuts a landscape of opportunity but a "mud track that wound up through the barren gravel hills and branched and broke and finally terminated in the tailings of an abandoned mine among the rusted shapes of pipe and pumpstanchions and old jacktimbers" (285). Instead of the promise and potential of starting life over an a Mexican hacienda, free from the taint of time and post-war industrialism, John Grady returns to a landscape he now sees as desolate, full of creosote and olive stands stretching back thousands of years. Instead of a "tenantless night" where the night sky, swarming with stars, is literally the limit, he finds "tenantless waste, older than any living thing that was" (285). Neither story presents a happy ending, yet Salinger's example continues to inspire readers and writers alike, young and old, who are drawn to the essential truths of growing up, seeking control, losing innocence, facing love and death for the first time. Holden and John Grady may remain broken and homeless at the end of their stories, but at least their experiences live on, finding refuge in classrooms, backpacks, nightstands and the hearts of readers, young and old, one hopes for many generations to come.

NOTES

1. Like Salinger, McCarthy has provided only one major published interview in his lifetime, with Richard B. Woodward for the *New York Times Magazine*. Elements of his biography and writing life are fleshed out further by Garry Wallace's "Meeting McCarthy" in the McCarthy special issue of *Southern Quarterly* and Marty Racine's more recent biographical review for the *Houston Chronicle*. Wallace, Woodward, and Racine all confirm that McCarthy favors Melville over any other author—and all find comparisons in both his fiction and his personal life to Hemingway. According to Wallace, McCarthy compared his reluctance to meet with the press to J. D. Salinger "who had given only one interview throughout his career as a novelist, to elementary children" (135).

McCarthy's confusion on this point suggests that he, at least, is not in league with the Salinger devotees who have intimate knowledge of every one of his authorized—and unauthorized—works, interviews, or rumors.

2. Also "All the Pretty Little Ponies," traditional, perhaps originating from slavery and the American South. See Diane Luce's discussion of the origins and possible significance of this lullaby in " 'When You Wake': John Grady Cole's Heroism in *All the Pretty Horses*." (156).

3. Portions of my analysis here are indebted to Terri Witek's discussion of homelessness and flight in "Reeds and Hides: Cormac McCarthy's Domestic Spaces" (136) and Tom Pilkington's discussion of "fate and free will" in Cormac McCarthy's fiction (320).

4. Portions of my analysis here are influenced by Robert L. Jarrett's discussion of the horse as "a rejection of the mechanized American Southwest of the post-World War II" (101) and John Grady's command and control of the horse as an attempt to bring nature to his will (108).

5. Peter Shaw elaborates this point in his essay, appropriate to our discussion here, "Love and Death in *The Catcher in the Rye*." The Burns poem and its popularization as a courtship song (or, to be more blunt in a modernistic vernacular, a "mating" song) have registered in Holden's head but only so far as it "implies the coming together of male and female bodies." Shaw argues that the second line of the poem "makes explicit the romantic/sexual content of the first." The fact that Holden "mishears" the first verse and never gets to the second, illustrates his frozen sexual development: "Unconsciously suppressing the word "meet," he avoids the very matter of his relations with girls, which he has been unable to resolve. 'Meet' acts as another reminder, like the 'fuck you' graffiti that keep confronting him, of the disturbing basis of love." (105).

6. Gerald Rosen makes a case that Holden links "time" and "sex" in this scene, particularly in the way he describes Stradlater "giving the time" to Jane, which has interesting implications in our earlier discussion of time and control (555).

7. Portions of my analysis here are influenced by Diane Luce (158) and Gail Moore Morrison (178-79) in their thorough analyses of the horse-breeding themes and the relations to sexuality and John Grady's initiation into adulthood.

8. Most of my analysis here is indebted to the concepts and ideas collected in Bert Bender's *The Descent of Love*, particularly his chapter on Hemingway's *The Sun Also Rises* (341-359).

9. This is precisely the point John M. Howell makes in connecting *Catcher* to T.S. Eliot, and this scene, specifically, with the "Burial of the Dead" section of *The Waste Land*. The influence of modernism is marked on Holden's narrative in a way that critics often ignore—seeing Holden suffering more from the weight of ego and immaturity than world-weariness and existentialism. Tom Pilkington identifies a similar dark vision in

All the Pretty Horses, noting that John Grady seeks independence and a sense of meaning and purpose but instead winds up with a "Hemingwayesque" understanding of his insignificance. By the end of the story, this mastery over nature and this hope and purpose in their escape lead to an "epiphany…that the individual is alone in a cold, indifferent universe" and that "the 'conceit of man' is that he continues to pit himself against the power of the elements, to assert his will against overwhelming force of nature. He continues to attempt to impose a moral order on a natural order—or, if Wallace Stevens is correct, a natural chaos—in which morality is irrelevant" (314).

WORKS CITED

Bender, Bert. *The Descent of Love: Darwin and the Theory of Sexual Selection in American Fiction, 1871–1926.* Philadelphia: U of Penn. P, 1996.

Fiedler, Leslie. *Love and Death in the American Novel.* New York: Anchor, 1992.

Howell, John M. "Salinger in the Waste Land." *Modern Fiction Studies* (J.D. Salinger Special Number) 12 (1966): 367–375.

Jarrett, Robert L. *Cormac McCarthy.* Twayne's United States Authors Series. New York: Twayne, 1997.

Luce, Diane. "'When You Wake:' John Grady Cole's Heroism in *All the Pretty Horses.*" *Sacred Violence: A Readers Companion to Cormac McCarthy.* Ed. Wade Hall and Rich Wallach. El Paso: Texas Western Press, 1995. 154–167.

McCarthy, Cormac. *All the Pretty Horses.* New York: First Vintage International Edition, 1993.

Morrison, Gail Moore. "*All the Pretty Horses:* John Grady Cole's Expulsion from Paradise" *Perspectives on Cormac McCarthy.* Ed. Edwin T. Arnold and Dianne C. Luce. Jackson: UP of Mississippi, 1993. 178–79.

Pilkington, Tom. "Fate and Free Will on the American Frontier: Cormac McCarthy's Western Fiction." *Western American Literature* 4 (1993): 311–322.

Racine, Marty. "Phantom on the Border." *Houston Chronicle*, 27 June 1999: 8–11.

Rosen, Gerald. "A Retrospective Look at *The Catcher in the Rye*." *American Quarterly* 24 (1977): 547–62.

Salinger J.D. *The Catcher in the Rye*. Boston: Little, Brown, 1951.

Shaw, Peter. "Love and Death in *The Catcher in the Rye*." *New Essays on* The Catcher in the Rye. Ed. Jack Salzman. New York: Cambridge UP, 1991. 97–114.

Wallace, Garry "Meeting McCarthy" *Southern Quarterly* 30:4 (1992): 134–139.

Witek, Terri. "Reeds and Hides: Cormac McCarthy's Domestic Spaces." *The Southern Review* 30.1 (1994): 136–142.

Woodward, Richard B. "Cormac McCarthy's Venomous Fiction." *New York Times Magazine*, 19 April 1992, late ed., sec. 6: 28+.

Bibliography

The following is a selected bibliography of *The Catcher in the Rye*. As such, it is concerned only with those works that are themselves concerned primarily with the novel. Works that focus their study primarily on J. D. Salinger or on Salinger's other stories and novellas—and which indeed may be relevant to a more thorough study of *The Catcher in the Rye*—nevertheless are not included herein.

Moreover, the following selection concentrates principally on studies and works of scholarship and criticism. Numerous reviews have been written of *The Catcher in the Rye*, but this bibliography lists only a few of these, which have been included only because they are cited by essays in this volume.

BOOKS

Bloom, Harold. *J. D. Salinger's* The Catcher in the Rye: *Bloom's Notes.* Broomall, PA: Chelsea House, 1996. 5–6.

——, ed. *Holden Caulfield.* Major Literary Characters Series. New York: Chelsea House, 1990.

Galloway, David D. *The Absurd Hero in American Fiction: Updike, Styron, Bellow, Salinger.* Austin: U of Texas P, 1966.

Grunwald, Henry Anatole, ed. *Salinger: A Critical and Personal Portrait.* New York: Pocket Books, 1963.

Hamilton, Ian. *In Search of J. D. Salinger.* New York: Random House, 1988.

Laser, Martin, and Norman Fruman, eds. *Studies in J.D. Salinger: Reviews, Essays, and Critiques of* The Catcher in the Rye *and Other Fiction*. New York: Odyssey Press, 1963.

Pinsker, Sanford. The Catcher in the Rye*: Innocence Under Pressure*. New York: Twayne, 1993.

Salzberg, Joel, ed. *Critical Essays on Salinger's* The Catcher in the Rye. Critical Essays on American Literature. Boston: G. K. Hall, 1990.

Salzman, Jack, ed. *New Essays on* The Catcher in the Rye. Cambridge: Cambridge UP, 1991.

Steinle, Pamela Hunt. *In Cold Fear:* The Catcher in the Rye*: Censorship Controversies and Postwar American Character*. Columbus, OH: Ohio State UP, 2000.

Sublette, Jack R. *J. D. Salinger: An Annotated Bibliography, 1938–81*. New York: Garland Publishing, 1984.

CHAPTERS, ARTICLES, AND REVIEWS

Barron, Cynthia M. "The Catcher and the Soldier: Hemingway's 'Soldier's Home' and Salinger's *The Catcher in the Rye*." *The Hemingway Review* 2.1 (Fall 1982): 70–73.

Baumbach, Jonathan. "The Saint as a Young Man: A Reappraisal of *The Catcher in the Rye*." *Modern Language Quarterly* 25:4 (December 1964): 461–72.

Bell, Barbara. "'Holden Caulfield in Doc Martens': *The Catcher in the Rye* and 'My So-Called Life.'" *Studies in Popular Culture* 19.1 (Oct. 1996): 47–57.

Bellman, Samuel I. "Peripheral (?) Characters in *Huckleberry Finn* and *Catcher in the Rye.*" *Mark Twain Journal* 19.1 (1977–78): 4–6.

Blei, Norbert. "If You Want to Know the Truth...: *The Catcher in the Rye.*" *Censored Books: Critical Viewpoints.* Ed. Nicholas Karolides, et al. Metuchen, NJ: Scarecrow, 1993. 159–66.

Bryan, James. "The Psychological Structure of *The Catcher in the Rye.*" *PMLA* 89 (1974): 1065–74.

———. "Sherwood Anderson and *The Catcher in the Rye*: A Possible Influence." *Notes on Contemporary Literature* 1.5 (1971): 2–6.

Burger, Nash K. "Books of *The Times.*" Review. *New York Times*, 16 July 1951: 19.

Burrows, David. "Allie and Phoebe: Death and Love in J. D. Salinger's *The Catcher in the Rye.*" *Private Dealings: Eight Modern American Writers.* Ed. David J. Burrows, et al. Stockholm: Almqvist & Wiksell, 1970. 106–14.

Cohen, Hubert I. "'A Woeful Agony Which Forced Me to Begin My Tale': *The Catcher in the Rye.*" *Modern Fiction Studies* 12 (Fall 1966): 355–66.

Dahl, James. "What About Antolini." *Notes on Contemporary Literature* 13.2 (Mar. 1983): 9–10.

Engle, Paul. "Honest Tale of Distraught Adolescent." Review. *Chicago Sunday Tribune Magazine of Books*, 15 July 1951: 3.

Fosburgh, Lacey. "J. D. Salinger Speaks About His Silence." *New York Times*, 3 Nov. 1974: 1A.

Hainsworth, J. D. "Maturity in J. D. Salinger's *The Catcher in the Rye*." *English Studies* 48 (1967): 426–31.

Howell, John M. "Salinger in the Waste Land." *Modern Fiction Studies* (J. D. Salinger Special Issue) 12 (1966): 367–375.

Huber, R. J. "Alderian Theory and Its Application to *The Catcher in the Rye*— Holden Caulfield." *Psychological Perspectives on Literature: Freudian Dissidents and Non-Freudians: A Casebook*. Ed. Joseph Natoli. Hamden, CT: Archon, 1984. 43–52.

Hughes, Riley. "New Novels." Review. *Catholic World* 1040 (Nov. 1951): 154.

Kinnick, Bernard C. "Holden Caulfield: Adolescents' Enduring Model." *High School Journal* 53: 8 (1970): 440–443.

Laser, Marvin. "Character Names in *The Catcher in the Rye*." *California English Journal* 1.1 (1965): 29–40.

Longstreth, T. Morris. "New Novels in the News." Review. *Christian Science Monitor* (19 July 1951): 11.

Lott, Sandra M., and Stephen Latham. "'The World Was All Before Them': Coming of Age in Ngugi wa Thiong'o's *Weep Not, Child* and J. D. Salinger's *The Catcher in the Rye*." *Global Perspectives on Teaching Literature: Shared Visions and Distinctive Visions*. Ed. Sandra Ward Lott, et al. Urbana, IL: Nat. Council of Teachers of Eng., 1993. 135–51.

Luedtke, Luther S. "J. D. Salinger and Robert Burns: *The Catcher in the Rye*." *Modern Fiction Studies* 16 (1970): 198–201.

Martin, Robert A. "Remembering Jane in *The Catcher in the Rye*." *Notes on Contemporary Literature* 28.4 (Sept. 1998): 2–3.

McClintock, James I. "*The Book of Daniel*: E. L. Doctorow's *The Catcher in the Rye*." *Notes on Contemporary Literature* 28.1 (Jan 1998): 6–8.

Medovoi, Leerom. "Democracy, Capitalism, and American Literature: The Cold War Construction of J. D. Salinger's Paperback Hero." *The Other Fifties: Interrogating Midcentury American Icons*. Ed. Joel Foreman. Urbana, IL: U of Illinois P, 1997. 255–87.

Miller, Edwin Haviland. "In Memoriam: Allie Caulfield." *Mosaic* 15:1 (Winter 1982): 129–40.

Miller, James E., Jr. "*Catcher* in and out of History." *Critical Inquiry* 3 (1977): 599–603.

Nadel, Alan. "Rhetoric, Sanity, and the Cold War: The Significance of Holden Caulfield's Testimony." *The Centennial Review* 32.4 (Fall 1988): 351–371.

Ohmann, Carol, and Richard Ohmann. "Reviewers, Critics and *The Catcher in the Rye*." *Critical Inquiry* 3 (1977): 15–37.

Pinsker, Sanford. "Catcher in the Rye and All: Is the Age of Formative Books Over?" *The Georgia Review* 50: 4 (1986): 953–967.

Roemer, Danielle M. "The Personal Narrative and Salinger's *Catcher in the Rye*." *Western Folklore* 51.1 (Jan. 1992): 5–10.

Rosen, Gerald. "A Retrospective Look at *The Catcher in the Rye.*" *American Quarterly* 24 (1977): 547–62.

Spanier, Sandra Whipple. "Hemingway's 'The Last Good Country' and *The Catcher in the Rye*: More Than a Family Resemblance." *Studies in Short Fiction* 19.1 (Winter 1982): 35–43.

Trowbridge, Clinton W. "Salinger's Symbolic Use of Character and Detail in *The Catcher in the Rye.*" *Cimarron Review* 4 (1968): 5–11.

Vanderbilt, Kermit. "Symbolic Resolution in *The Catcher in the Rye*: The Cap, the Carrousel and the American West." *Western Humanities Review* 17 (1963): 271–277.

Whitfield, Stephen J. "Cherished and Cursed: Toward a Social History of *The Catcher in the Rye.*" *New England Quarterly* 70.4 (Dec. 1997): 567–600.

Zapf, Hubert. "Logical Action in *The Catcher in the Rye.*" *College Literature* 12.3 (Fall 1985): 266–271.

Contributors

J. P. STEED teaches at Western Oregon University. He has published articles on authors such as Bernard Malamud, Raymond Carver, and Francine Prose, and his current project is a collection of essays on humor and identity in American Jewish fiction.

MARK SILVERBERG has published on twentieth-century literature and culture in journals such as *English Studies in Canada, Dalhousie Review, Essays on Canadian Writing,* and *Arizona Quarterly* (forthcoming). He teaches at Dalhousie University and at St. Mary's University in Halifax, Nova Scotia.

ROBERT MILTNER teaches at Kent State University, Stark. He is the author of *Salinger's "The Catcher in the Rye"* (Center for Learning, 1988). His reviews, fictions, and poems have appeared in *Pleiades, Poetry International, Mochila Review, CrossConnect, Barrow Street, Montserrat Review,* and *EnterText.* His chapbook, *Against the Simple,* won a Wick Chapbook Award.

DENNIS CUTCHINS is an associate professor of English at Brigham Young University, where he teaches American and Western literature as well as film and literature. He earned his Ph.D. from the Florida State University and has published articles on Native American literature and Utah folklore.

JOSEPH S. WALKER teaches at Auburn University, where he is at work on a book examining the functions of crime in contemporary American fiction and film. His work has appeared in *Modern Fiction Studies* and *The Centennial Review.*

MATT EVERTSON is an Instructor in the Department of Language and Literature at Chadron State College in Nebraska and a Ph.D. candidate in American literature at Arizona State University. He is currently working on a comparative study of the writings of Stephen Crane and Theodore Roosevelt.

Index